Vintage Knitwear

for Modern Knitters

Lise-Lotte Lystrup

Vintage Knitwear
for Modern Knitters

with 101 illustrations, 67 in color

Thames & Hudson

First published in 2008 in paperback in the United States of
America by Thames & Hudson Inc., 500 Fifth Avenue,
New York, New York 10110

thamesandhudsonusa.com

Library of Congress Catalog Card Number 2008901141

ISBN 978-0-500-28756-9

Printed and bound in Singapore by CS Graphics

CONTENTS

Introduction 7

Introduction

After twenty years in which it seemed that nobody was learning to knit any more, suddenly knitting is back in fashion everywhere. Knitting classes and forums are mushrooming. A great many teenage girls (and boys) are knitting whenever possible, while at lots of colleges it seems as if the whole campus is knitting. There are even knitting events being held at cinemas and nightclubs across the US and UK.

Hand in hand with this newfound passion for vintage craft is a rediscovery of vintage design. A great deal of knitwear from the 1930s to 1950s was of such exquisite design that it would be hard to better. Vintage garments for women were wonderfully feminine, flattering and snug. However the truth is that old patterns can be intimidating and disappointing. The beautiful pictures and elegant styles are irresistibly enticing, but to translate the instructions into garments that can be worn today is another matter altogether. People generally now are bigger than they were fifty to seventy years ago, so that most patterns from that period only give sizes that today are classed as small or very small. The different yarns used then created totally different gauges from yarns available today. Many vintage patterns are not only highly intricate and demanding, they are also frequently inadequate and faulty. I have often wondered how anyone managed to create a garment at all in those days.

In my work recreating authentic vintage knitwear for period productions on film, stage and television I have encountered and overcome such difficulties many times. Consequently I have totally redesigned all the patterns in this book to fit women today, and to make them easy to knit using readily available modern yarns.

The choice of patterns here represents those that have inspired me most – the ones that have made me want to grab my needles and that I couldn't wait to see finished. I hope you will feel the same way. To help you choose a pattern to match your skills, they are graded with one to three balls of yarn: one ball for the novice knitter, two for the slightly more advanced, and three for the expert. Techniques and abbreviations are explained at the back of the book (pages 91–92). So whether you are new to the delights of the craft or are an experienced knitter looking for fresh inspiration, there is something here for you. I wish you many wonderful hours of knitting.

Lise-Lotte Lystrup

Evening Jacket in Feather Pattern

Lamé sparkle and swansdown trim make this a jewel of a jacket!

FINISHED MEASUREMENTS

To fit bust 32 (34, 36, 38, 40, 42)" / 81 (86, 91, 97, 102, 107) cm

Length 21½ (22½, 23½, 24½, 25½, 26)" / 55 (57, 60, 62, 65, 66) cm

Sleeve seam length 17¾ (17¾, 18, 18, 18, 18½)" / 45 (45, 46, 46, 46, 47) cm

MATERIALS

6 (6, 7, 7, 8, 8) 50g balls of Capricorn Mohair, Superfine Brushed 4 Ply in 115 Navy

1 250g cone of Yeoman Yarns, Manila Lamé 2 ply in 11 Navy

1 pair size 8 US / 5mm needles

60" / 1.5 metre swansdown trim

GAUGE / TENSION

22 sts and 24 rows = 4" / 10 cm in pattern using size 8 US / 5mm needles

The entire jacket is knitted with one strand of mohair and one strand of lamé combined.

PATTERN

Row 1 K2tog, K2tog, * (yo / yrn, K1) 3 times, yo / yrn, (K2tog) 4 times, rep from * till 7 sts rem, (yo / yrn, K1) 3 times, yo / yrn, K2tog, K2tog.
Row 2 P.
Row 3 K.
Row 4 K.

The entire Jacket is worked in this pattern, apart from the first 2 rows on Back, Fronts and Sleeves.

BACK

Cast on 99 (99, 110, 110, 121, 121) sts.

K first 2 rows and cont even / straight in patt till Back meas 15 (15¾, 16½, 17¼, 18, 18½)" / 38 (40, 42, 44, 46, 47) cm.

Shape armholes

Bind / cast off 3 sts at beg of next 2 rows.

K2tog at beg and end of next and every row till there are 77 (77, 77, 88, 88, 88) sts on needle.

Cont even / straight till Back meas 21½ (22½, 23½, 24½, 25½, 26)" / 55 (57, 60, 62, 65, 66) cm.

Bind / cast off 26 (26, 26, 30, 30, 30) sts at beg of next 2 rows for shoulders.

Bind / cast off the rem 25 (25, 25, 28, 28, 28) sts.

RIGHT FRONT

Cast on 44 (44, 55, 55, 66, 66) sts.

K first 2 rows and cont even / straight in patt till Front meas 15 (15¾, 16½, 17¼, 18, 18½)" / 38 (40, 42, 44, 46, 47) cm.

Shape armholes

Next row (WS) Bind / cast off 3 sts at beg of row.

K2tog on every row at armhole edge till there are 26 (26, 26, 30, 30, 30) sts on needle.

Cont even / straight till Front meas 21½ (22½, 23½, 24½, 25½, 26)" / 55 (57, 60, 62, 65, 66) cm.

Bind / cast off.

LEFT FRONT

Work as for Right Front, but rev the shapings.

SLEEVES (both alike)

Cast on 77 (77, 88, 88, 99, 99) sts.

K first 2 rows and cont even / straight in patt till Sleeve meas 17¾ (17¾, 18, 18, 18, 18½)" / 45 (45, 46, 46, 46, 47) cm.

Shape top

Bind / cast off 3 sts at beg of next 2 rows.

K2 tog at beg and end of every row till there are 23 (23, 22, 22, 29, 29) sts on needle.

Bind / cast off.

FINISHING

Press lightly and join all seams.

Sew swansdown along neck and down fronts.

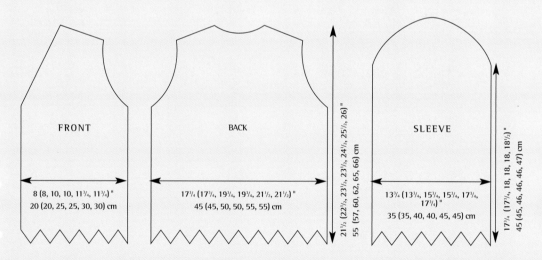

FRONT

8 (8, 10, 10, 11¾, 11¾)"
20 (20, 25, 25, 30, 30) cm

BACK

17¾ (17¾, 19¾, 19¾, 21½, 21½)"
45 (45, 50, 50, 55, 55) cm

21½ (22½, 23¾, 23¾, 24½, 25½, 26)"
55 (57, 60, 62, 65, 66) cm

SLEEVE

13¾ (13¾, 15¾, 15¾, 17¾, 17¾)"
35 (35, 40, 40, 45, 45) cm

17¼ (17¼, 18, 18, 18, 18½)"
45 (45, 46, 46, 46, 47) cm

1933

Jacket with Frog Fasteners

A snug, figure-hugging jacket, perfect for smart outings in town.

FINISHED MEASUREMENTS

To fit bust 32 (34, 36, 38, 40, 42)" / 81 (86, 91, 97, 102, 107) cm

Length 21½ (22½, 23½, 24½, 25½, 26½)" / 55 (57, 60, 62, 65, 67) cm

Sleeve seam length 17¾ (17¾, 18, 18, 18, 18½)" / 45 (45, 46, 46, 46, 47) cm

MATERIALS

15 (15, 16, 16, 17, 17) 50g balls of Yeoman Yarns, Mondial, Artico in 147 Olive

1 pair size 9 US / 5.5mm needles

1 pair size 10 US / 6mm needles

1 stitch holder

6 large frog fasteners (use only half of the pair)

1 transparent snap fastener

GAUGE / TENSION

16 sts and 24 rows = 4" / 10 cm in pattern using size 10 US / 6mm needles

PATTERN (Divisible by 6 sts)

Row 1 (RS) K.
Row 2 (K2, P4) till end.
Row 3 K3, P2, (K4, P2) till 1 st rem, K1.
Row 4 P.
Row 5 (P2, K4) till end.
Row 6 P3, K2, (P4, K2) till 1 st rem, P1.

The entire Jacket is worked in this pattern, apart from the cuffs, front border and Collar.

BACK

With size 10 US / 6mm needles cast on 66 (70, 74, 78, 82, 86) sts.

Work in patt, incorporating the odd sts as follows:
Row 1 (RS) K.
Row 2 (K2, P4) till 0 (4, 2, 0, 4, 2) sts rem, K0 (2, 2, 0, 2, 2), P0 (2, 0, 0, 2, 0).
Row 3 K0 (1, 0, 0, 1, 0), P0 (2, 1, 0, 2, 1), K3 (4, 4, 3, 4, 4), P2, (K4, P2) till 1 st rem, K1.
Row 4 P.
Row 5 (P2, K4) till 0 (4, 2, 0, 4, 2) sts rem, P0 (2, 2, 0, 2, 2), K0 (2, 0, 0, 2, 0).
Row 6 P0 (1, 0, 0, 1, 0), K0 (2, 1, 0, 2, 1), P3 (4, 4, 3, 4, 4), K2, (P4, K2) till 1 st rem, P1.

Cont even / straight till work meas 5½ (6, 6¼, 6¾, 7¼, 7½)" / 14 (15, 16, 17, 18, 19) cm or length required till 1" / 2.5 cm before waist.

Change to size 9 US / 5.5mm needles.

Work 12 rows in patt.

Change to size 10 US / 6mm needles.

Cont even / straight till Back meas 15 (15¾, 16½, 17¼, 18, 19)" / 38 (40, 42, 44, 46, 48) cm or length required to armhole.

Shape armholes

Bind / cast off 4 (4, 4, 5, 5, 5) sts at beg of next 2 rows.

Bind / cast off 2 (2, 3, 3, 4, 4) sts at beg of next 2 rows.

Bind / cast off 1 (2, 2, 2, 2, 2) sts at beg of next 2 rows.

Bind / cast off 1 (1, 1, 1, 1, 2) sts at beg of next 2 rows.

Dec 1 st at beg of next 4 rows [46 (48, 50, 52, 54, 56) sts].

Cont even / straight till Back meas 21 (21$\frac{1}{2}$, 22$\frac{3}{4}$, 23$\frac{1}{2}$, 24$\frac{3}{4}$, 25$\frac{1}{2}$)" / 53 (55, 58, 60, 63, 65) cm.

Shape shoulders

Bind / cast off 5 sts at beg of next 2 rows.

Bind / cast off 5 (5, 5, 5, 6, 6) sts at beg of next 2 rows.

Bind / cast off 5 (5, 6, 6, 6, 6) sts at beg of next 2 rows.

Slip the rem 16 (18, 18, 20, 20, 22) sts onto a st holder.

RIGHT FRONT

With size 10 US / 6mm needles cast on 48 (51, 54, 58, 61, 64) sts.

Row 1 (RS) K.
Row 2 Work in patt till 6 sts rem, K6.
Row 3 K6, work in patt to end.

Cont even / straight in patt working a border of 6 g-st.

Cont in patt as for Back (changing to smaller needles at the waist) till work meas 15 (15$\frac{3}{4}$, 16$\frac{1}{2}$, 17$\frac{1}{4}$, 18, 19)" / 38 (40, 42, 44, 46, 48) cm.

Shape armhole

Row 1 (WS) Bind / cast off 4 (4, 4, 5, 5, 5) st at beg of row.
Row 2 and every alt row Work in patt.

Row 3 Bind / cast off 2 (2, 3, 3, 4, 4) sts at beg of row.
Row 5 Bind / cast off 1 (2, 2, 2, 2, 2) sts at beg of row.
Row 7 Bind / cast off 1 (1, 1, 1, 1, 2) sts at beg of row.
Row 9 and 11 Dec 1 st at beg of row [38 (40, 42, 45, 47, 49) sts].

Cont even / straight in patt till Front meas 19$\frac{3}{4}$ (20, 21$\frac{1}{2}$, 22$\frac{1}{2}$, 23$\frac{1}{2}$, 24$\frac{1}{2}$)" / 50 (52, 55, 57, 60, 62) cm.

Jacket with Frog Fasteners

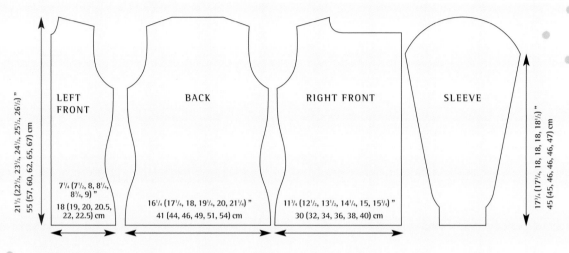

21¹/₂ (22¹/₂, 23¹/₂, 24¹/₂, 25¹/₂, 26¹/₂) "
55 (57, 60, 62, 65, 67) cm

LEFT
FRONT

7¹/₄ (7¹/₂, 8, 8¹/₄, 8³/₄, 9) "
18 (19, 20, 20.5, 22, 22.5) cm

BACK

16¹/₄ (17¹/₄, 18, 19¹/₂, 20, 21¹/₄) "
41 (44, 46, 49, 51, 54) cm

RIGHT FRONT

11³/₄ (12¹/₂, 13¹/₂, 14¹/₄, 15, 15³/₄) "
30 (32, 34, 36, 38, 40) cm

SLEEVE

17¹/₄ (17¹/₄, 18, 18, 18¹/₂) "
45 (45, 46, 46, 46, 47) cm

Shape neck

Row 1 (RS) Bind / cast off 19 (21, 22, 25, 26, 28) sts, work in patt to end.
Row 2 and 4 Work in patt till 2 sts rem, K2tog.
Row 3 and 5 K2tog, work in patt to end.

Work 2 rows in patt.

Shape shoulder

Row 1 Bind / cast off 5 sts, work in patt to end.
Row 2 and 4 Work in patt.
Row 3 Bind / cast off 5 (5, 5, 5, 6, 6) sts, work in patt to end.

Bind / cast off the rem 5 (5, 6, 6, 6, 6) sts.

LEFT FRONT

With size 10 US / 6mm needles cast on 29 (30, 32, 33, 35, 36) sts.

Proceed as for Right Front keeping a 6 sts g-st border at front edge till work meas 15 (15³/₄, 16¹/₂, 17¹/₄, 18, 19)" / 38 (40, 42, 44, 46, 48) cm.

Shape armhole

Row 1 (RS) Bind / cast off 4 (4, 4, 5, 5, 5) sts at beg of row.
Row 2 and every alt row Work in patt.
Row 3 Bind / cast off 2 (2, 3, 3, 4, 4) sts at beg of row.
Row 5 Bind / cast off 1 (2, 2, 2, 2, 2) sts at beg of row.
Row 7 Bind / cast off 1 (1, 1, 1, 1, 2) sts at beg of row.
Row 9 and 11 Dec 1 st at beg of row [19 (19, 20, 20, 21, 21) sts].

Cont even / straight till Front meas 19³/₄ (20, 21¹/₂, 22¹/₂, 23¹/₂, 24¹/₂)" / 50 (52, 55, 57, 60, 62) cm.

Shape neck

Row 1 and 3 (RS) Work in patt till 2 sts rem, K2tog.
Row 2 and 4 K2tog, work in patt to end.

Work 2 rows in patt.

Shape shoulder

Row 1 Bind / cast off 5 sts, work in patt to end.
Row 2 and 4 Work in patt.
Row 3 Bind / cast off 5 (5, 5, 5, 6, 6) sts, work in patt to end.

Bind / cast off the rem 5 (5, 6, 6, 6, 6) sts.

SLEEVES (both alike)

With size 9 US / 5.5mm needles cast on 26 (28, 30, 32, 34, 36) sts.

Work in rib of K1, P1 for 2" / 5 cm.

Change to size 10 US / 6mm needles.

Cont in patt and inc 1 st at beg and end of every 8th row 11 (11, 11, 10, 10, 10) times till there are 48 (50, 52, 52, 54, 56) sts on needle.

Cont even / straight in patt till sleeve meas $17^3/_4$ ($17^3/_4$, 18, 18, $18^1/_2$)" / 45 (45, 46, 46, 46, 47) cm or length required.

Shape top

Bind / cast off 2 (3, 3, 3, 3, 3) sts at beg of next 2 rows.

Bind / cast off 2 sts at beg of next 2 rows.

K2tog at beg and end of every alt row till 12 (14, 14, 14, 14, 16) sts rem.

Bind / cast off the rem sts.

FINISHING

Press all pieces lightly.

Sew shoulder, side and sleeve seams.

Sew in sleeves.

COLLAR

With RS facing, using size 9 US / 5.5mm needles pick up and knit 16 sts on Right Front from dec at top, 16 (18, 18, 20, 20, 22) sts on Back, 16 sts on Left Front [48 (50, 50, 52, 52, 54) sts].

1936

Work in rib of K1, P1 for 3 rows.

Next row Inc 1 st, work in rib till 1 st rem, inc 1 st.

Work 3 rows in rib.

Rep last 4 rows till Collar meas 4" / 10 cm.

Bind / cast off loosely in rib.

FASTENINGS

Detach button from frog. Sew frog on Right Front and button to correspond on Left Front.

Sew on snap fastener at neck.

3 V-Striped Scarf

FINISHED MEASUREMENTS

Length without tassels 76" / 193 cm

Width 6" / 15 cm

MATERIALS

1 50 g ball of each of Yeoman Yarns, Sport in 4 Red, 24 Royal, 23 Emerald, 156 Tangerine, 20 Oatmeal

1 50 g ball of Yeoman Yarns, Fifty Fifty in 8 Midas (yellow)

1 pair size 5 US / 3.75mm needles

1 pair size 6 US / 4mm needles

1 crochet hook size E / 3.5mm

GAUGE / TENSION

24 sts and 46 rows = 4" / 10 cm using size 6 US / 4mm needles

The entire scarf is knitted in g-st.

SCARF

With size 6 US / 4mm needles cast on 50 sts with Red.

Row 1 K.
Row 2 K1, M1, K22, K2tog, K2tog, K22, M1, K1.

Rep these 2 rows 5 more times.

Change to size 5 US / 3.75mm needles and Midas. Knit the Midas with 2 strands throughout scarf. Rep the first 2 rows 6 times.

Change to size 6 US / 4mm needles and Royal. Rep the first 2 rows 6 times.

Change to Emerald. Rep the first 2 rows 6 times.

Change to Tangerine. Rep the first 2 rows 6 times.

Change to Oatmeal. Rep the first 2 rows 6 times.

Rep this set of colours 3 more times.

Middle square

Change to Red.

Row 1 K50.
Row 2 K27, turn.
Row 3 K3, K2tog, turn.
Row 4 K4, K2tog, turn.
Row 5 K5, K2tog, turn.
Row 6 K6, K2tog, turn.

1930–39

Row 7   K7, K2tog, turn.
Row 8   K8, K2tog, turn.
Row 9   K9, K2tog, turn.
Row 10   K10, K2tog, turn.
Row 11   K11, K2tog, turn.
Row 12   K13, turn.
Row 13   K15, turn.
Row 14   K15, K2tog, turn.
Row 15   K16, K2tog, turn.
Row 16   K17, K2tog, turn.
Row 17   K18, K2tog, turn.
Row 18   K21, turn.
Row 19   K21, K2tog, turn.
Row 20   K22, K2tog, turn.
Row 21   K23, K2tog, turn.
Row 22   K24, K2tog, turn.
Row 23   K25, K2tog, turn.
Row 24   K27, turn.
Row 25   K28, turn.
Row 26   K29, turn.
Row 27   K30, turn.
Row 28   K32, turn.
Row 29   K30, turn.
Row 30   K29, turn.

Row 31   K28, turn.
Row 32   K27, turn.
Row 33   K24, M1, K1, turn.
Row 34   K23, M1, K1, turn.
Row 35   K22, M1, K1, turn.
Row 36   K21, M1, K1, turn.
Row 37   K20, M1, K1, turn.
Row 38   K21, turn.
Row 39   K17, M1, K1, turn.
Row 40   K16, M1, K1, turn.
Row 41   K15, M1, K1, turn.
Row 42   K14, M1, K1, turn.
Row 43   K15, turn.
Row 44   K13, turn.
Row 45   K10, M1, K1, turn.
Row 46   K9, M1, K1, turn.
Row 47   K8, M1, K1, turn.
Row 48   K7, M1, K1, turn.
Row 49   K6, M1, K1, turn.
Row 50   K5, M1, K1, turn.
Row 51   K4, M1, K1, turn.
Row 52   K3, M1, K1, turn.
Row 53   K2, M1, K1, turn.
Row 54   K2, turn.
Row 55   K27, turn.
Row 56   K50.

Change to Oatmeal.

Row 1   K.
Row 2   K1, K2tog, K22, M1, M1, K22, K2tog, K1.

Rep these last 2 rows 5 more times.

Change to Tangerine.
Rep the last 2 rows 6 times.

Change to Emerald.
Rep the last 2 rows 6 times.

Change to Royal.
Rep the last 2 rows 6 times.

Change to size 5 US / 3.75mm needles and Midas.
Rep the last 2 rows 6 times.

Change to size 6 US / 4mm needles and Red.
Rep the last 2 rows 6 times

Rep this set of colours 3 more times.

Bind / cast off.

FINISHING

Crochet a border of sc / dc around entire scarf in Red.

Make 2 large tassels in Red (see page 92) and attach one to each end of scarf.

6" / 15 cm

76" / 193 cm

Sports Sweater in Basket Weave

You'll look just the part on the golf course or at the tennis club.

FINISHED MEASUREMENTS

To fit bust 32 (34, 36, 38, 40, 42)" / 81 (86, 91, 97, 102, 107) cm

Length 22³⁄₄ (23¹⁄₄, 23³⁄₄, 24, 24¹⁄₂, 24³⁄₄)" / 58 (59, 60, 61, 62, 63) cm

Sleeve seam length 17³⁄₄ (17³⁄₄, 18, 18, 18, 18¹⁄₂)" / 45 (45, 46, 46, 46, 47) cm

MATERIALS

15 (15, 16, 16, 17, 17) 50g balls of Yeoman Yarns, Mondial, Artico in 600 Grey

1 50g ball of Mondial, Artico in 200 Black

1 pair size 7 US / 4.5mm needles

1 pair size 9 US / 5.5mm needles

1 crochet hook size E / 3.5mm

3 stitch holders

GAUGE / TENSION

16 sts and 20 rows = 4" / 10 cm in pattern using size 9 US / 5.5mm needles

PATTERN

Row 1 K.
Row 2 P.
Row 3 *P2, K2, rep from * to end.
Row 4 *K2, P2, rep from * to end.
Row 5 *P2 K2, rep from * to end.
Row 6 *K2, P2, rep from * to end.
Row 7 K.
Row 8 P.
Row 9 *K2, P2, rep from * to end.
Row 10 *P2, K2, rep from * to end.
Row 11 *K2, P2, rep from * to end.
Row 12 *P2, K2, rep from * to end.

The entire Sweater is worked in this pattern apart from the ribbing on Front and Back, the cuffs on the Sleeves, the front closure and the neckband.

BACK

With size 7 US / 4.5mm needles cast on 74 (78, 82, 86, 90, 94) sts.

Work in rib of K2, P2 for 4" / 10 cm.

Change to size 9 US / 5.5mm needles and cont even / straight in patt till Back meas 14¹⁄₄ (14¹⁄₂, 15¹⁄₄, 15³⁄₄, 16¹⁄₂, 17)" / 36 (37, 39, 40, 42, 43) cm or length required to armhole.

Shape armholes

Row 1 and 2 Bind / cast off 3 (3, 4, 4, 4, 5) sts at beg of row.
Row 3 and 4 Bind / cast off 2 (2, 3, 3, 3, 4) sts at beg of row.

4 Sports Sweater in Basket Weave

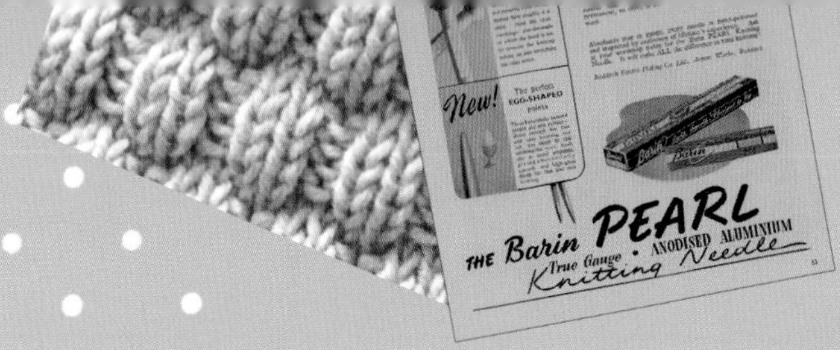
New!
THE Barin PEARL
True Gauge • ANODISED ALUMINIUM
Knitting Needle

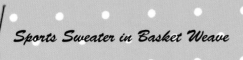

Row 5 and 6 Bind / cast off 1 (1, 2, 2, 2, 3) sts at beg of row.
Row 7 and 8 Bind / cast off 1 (1, 1, 1, 2, 1) sts at beg of row.
Row 9, 11 and 13 Work even / straight.
Row 10 Dec 1 st at beg and end of row.
Row 12 Dec 1 (1, 0, 1, 1, 1) st at beg and end of row.
Row 14 Dec 0 (1, 0, 1, 1, 0) st at beg and end of row [56 (58, 60, 60, 62, 64) sts].

Work even / straight till Back meas 22¾ (23¼, 24, 24½, 25¼, 25½)" / 58 (59, 61, 62, 64, 65) cm.

Shape shoulders

Bind / cast off 16 (16, 17, 17, 18, 18) sts, work 24 (26, 26, 26, 26, 28) sts in patt, bind / cast off 16 (16, 17, 17, 18, 18) sts.

Slip the rem 24 (26, 26, 26, 26, 28) sts onto a st holder.

FRONT

Work as for Back till Front meas 12½ (12½, 13½, 13¾, 14½, 15¼)" / 32 (32, 34, 35, 37, 38) cm.

Next row (RS) Work 29 (31, 33, 35, 37, 39) sts in patt, K16, patt 29 (31, 33, 35, 37, 39) sts.

Work 3 rows more in patt, keeping the 16 centre sts in g-st.

Divide for neck

Next row (RS) Work 29 (31, 33, 35, 37, 39) sts in patt, K8, turn.

Work 3 rows more in patt on these 37 (39, 41, 43, 45, 47) sts, keeping 8 sts at front edge in g-st.

Next row Work in patt till 6 sts rem, K2tog, yo / yrn, K4. A buttonhole has now been made.

Make 5 more buttonholes in the same way on every 10th row. **At the same time**, when Front meas 14¼ (14½, 15¼, 15¾, 16½, 17)" / 36 (37, 39, 40, 42, 43) cm, shape armhole as follows:

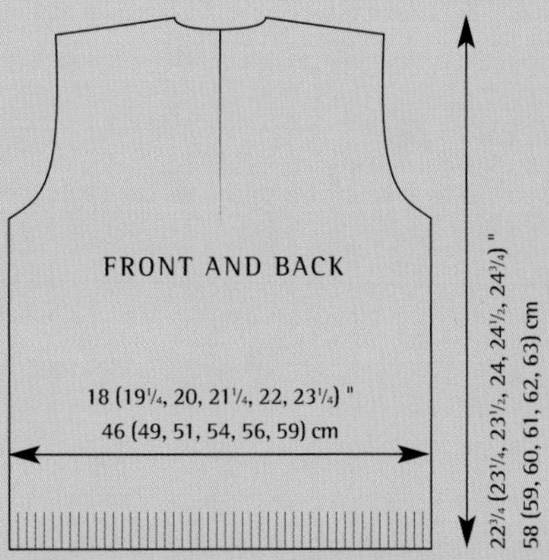
FRONT AND BACK
18 (19¼, 20, 21¼, 22, 23¼) "
46 (49, 51, 54, 56, 59) cm
22¾ (23¼, 23½, 24, 24½, 24¾) "
58 (59, 60, 61, 62, 63) cm

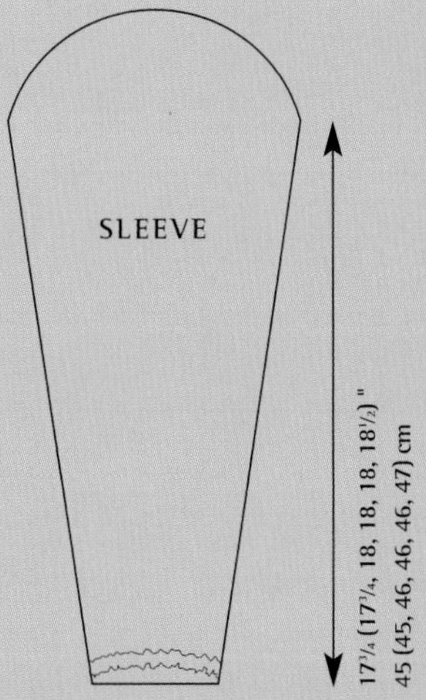
SLEEVE
17¼ (17¼, 18, 18, 18, 18½) "
45 (45, 46, 46, 46, 47) cm

1936

Shape armhole

Row 1 (RS) Bind / cast off 3 (3, 4, 4, 4, 5) sts at beg of row.

Row 2 and every alt row Work even / straight.

Row 3 Bind / cast off 2 (2, 3, 3, 3, 4) sts at beg of row.

Row 5 Bind / cast off 1 (1, 2, 2, 2, 3) sts at beg of row.

Row 7 Bind / cast off 1 (1, 1, 1, 2, 1) sts at beg of row.

Row 9 Dec 1 st at beg of row.

Row 11 Dec 1 (1, 0, 1, 1, 1) st at beg of row.

Row 13 Dec 0 (1, 0, 1, 1, 0) st at beg of row [28 (29, 30, 30, 31, 32) sts].

When Front meas 21½ (22, 22¾, 23¼, 24, 24½)" / 55 (56, 58, 59, 61, 62) cm, shape neck as follows:

Shape neck

Row 1 (WS) K8 and pass onto st holder, work in patt to end.

Row 2 and 4 Work in patt to last 2 sts, K2tog.

Row 3 and 5 K2tog, work in patt to end.

Row 6 Work in patt to last 0 (2, 2, 2, 2, 2) sts, K0tog (K2tog, K2tog, K2tog, K2tog, K2 tog).

Row 7 Work even / straight.

Bind / cast off the rem 16 (16, 17, 17, 18, 18) sts.

Join yarn to the centre front on the opposite side and finish this side to match the left.

Sew the back and front shoulders tog.

NECKBAND

RS With size 7 US / 4.5mm needles pick up and knit 8 sts from Right Front st holder, 5 sts up Right Front, 24 (26, 26, 26, 26, 28) sts from Back st holder, 5 sts down Left Front, and 8 sts from Left Front st holder [50 (52, 52, 52, 52, 54) sts].

Work 5 rows in g-st.

Next row (RS) K4, yo / yrn, K2tog, K till 6 sts rem, K2tog, yo / yrn, K4.

Work 5 rows in g-st.

Bind / cast off.

SLEEVES (both alike)

With size 7 US / 4.5mm needles cast on 15 (16, 17, 17, 18, 19) sts.

Work 6 rows in g-st.

Row 7 K4, yo / yrn, K2tog, K9 (10, 11, 11, 12, 13) sts.

Work 3 rows in g-st.

Cut yarn.

On the same needle cast on 15 (16, 17, 17, 18, 19) sts.

Work 6 rows in g-st.

Row 7 K9 (10, 11, 11, 12, 13), K2tog, yo / yrn, K4.

Work 3 rows in g-st.

Row 11 K right across the sts of both pieces, then work 5 rows more in g-st across all sts.

Change to size 9 US / 5.5mm needles and work 6 rows in patt.

Inc 1 st at both ends of next and every foll 6th row working extra sts into patt till there are 52 (54, 56, 56, 58, 60) sts in all.

Cont even / straight in patt till Sleeve meas 17³⁄₄ (17³⁄₄, 18, 18, 18, 18¹⁄₂)" / 45 (45, 46, 46, 46, 47) cm.

Shape top

Dec 1 st at beg and end of every alt row till 22 (24, 24, 24, 24, 26) sts rem.

Bind / cast off.

FINISHING

Sew in the sleeves.

Sew up the side seams.

DOUBLE BUTTON-LOOPS
(make 8)

With black yarn and the crochet hook, work 70 ch and join into a ring.

Fold this into a double piece and make a knot at each end.

Pass these knots through the holes on each side of the front and on the cuffs of the sleeves.

Cardigan with Contrasting Collar

Smart career girls will love this crisp nautical colour combination. Ahoy!

FINISHED MEASUREMENTS

To fit bust 32 (34, 36, 38, 40, 42)" / 81 (86, 91, 97, 102, 107) cm

Length 21½ (22½, 23½, 24½, 25½, 26½)" / 55 (57, 60, 62, 65, 67) cm

Sleeve seam length 17¾ (17¾, 18, 18, 18, 18½)" / 45 (45, 46, 46, 46, 47) cm

MATERIALS

8 (8, 9, 9, 10, 10) 50g balls of Jaeger Matchmaker Merino 4 ply in 698 Indigo.

2 50g balls of Jaeger Matchmaker Merino 4 ply in 661 White.

1 pair size 3 US / 3.25mm needles

1 pair size 5 US / 3.75mm needles

3 stitch holders

3 large and 2 small buttons

GAUGE / TENSION

26 sts and 34 rows = 4" / 10 cm in patt using size 5 US / 3.75mm needles

26 sts and 32 rows = 4" / 10 cm in st st using size 5 US / 3.75mm needles

PATTERN

Row 1 (RS) * K3, sl 1, rep from * to end.
Row 2 P.

BACK

With size 5 US / 3.75mm needles and Indigo yarn cast on 118 (124, 130, 138, 146, 152) sts and work even / straight in patt for 2" / 5 cm.

K2tog at beg and end of next row and every 4th row 8 times.

Work even / straight in patt for 2" / 5 cm.

Inc 1 st at beg and end of next row and every 6th row till there are 118 (124, 130, 138, 146, 152) sts on needle.

Work even / straight in patt till Back meas 15 (15¾, 16½, 17¼, 18, 19)" / 38 (40, 42, 44, 46, 48) cm or length required to armhole.

Shape armholes

Bind / cast off 6 sts at beg of next 2 rows.

Bind / cast off 3 (3, 4, 5, 5, 5) sts at beg of next 2 rows.

Bind / cast off 2 (2, 2, 3, 4, 4) sts at beg of next 2 rows.

Bind / cast off 1 (1, 1, 2, 2, 3) sts at beg of next 2 rows.

Bind / cast off 1 (1, 1, 2, 2, 2) sts at beg of next 2 rows.

Bind / cast off 1 (1, 1, 1, 1, 2) sts at beg of next 2 rows.

Bind / cast off 0 (1, 1, 1, 1, 1) sts at beg of next 2 rows.

1930–39

Bind / cast off 0 (0, 1, 0, 1, 1) sts at beg of next 2 rows [90 (94, 96, 98, 102, 104) sts rem].

Work even / straight in patt till Back meas 21 (21$\frac{1}{2}$, 22$\frac{3}{4}$, 23$\frac{1}{2}$, 24$\frac{3}{4}$, 25$\frac{1}{2}$)" / 53 (55, 58, 60, 63, 65) cm.

Shape shoulders

Bind / cast off 6 (6, 6, 7, 7, 7) sts at beg of next 2 rows.

Bind / cast off 6 (6, 6, 6, 7, 7) sts at beg of next 2 rows.

Bind / cast off 6 sts at beg of next 4 rows.

Bind / cast off rem 42 (46, 48, 48, 50, 52) sts.

POCKET LINING (make 2)

With Indigo yarn and size 5 US / 3.75mm needles cast on 31 sts and work even / straight in patt for 4" / 10 cm.

Slip sts onto a st holder and cut yarn.

LEFT FRONT

With size 5 US / 3.75mm needles and Indigo yarn cast on 65 (66, 68, 72, 75, 77) sts and work even / straight in patt for 2" / 5 cm.

K2tog at beg of next row (RS) and every 4th row 8 times, to shape side edge. **At the same time**, when work meas 4" / 10 cm, insert the pocket as follows:

Next row (RS) Work in patt till 51 sts rem, slip the next 31 sts onto a st holder, work the rem 20 sts in patt.

Next row P20, then, with the WS of one of the pockets facing you, P31 sts from pocket, P to end of row.

** Work even / straight for 2" (5 cm).

Inc 1 st at beg of next and every 8th row till there are 65 (66, 68, 72, 75, 77) sts on needle.

Cont without further shaping at side edge till Front meas 15 (15$\frac{3}{4}$, 16$\frac{1}{2}$, 17$\frac{1}{4}$, 18, 19)" / 38 (40, 42, 44, 46, 48) cm or length required to armhole. **At the same time** when front edge meas 11 (11$\frac{3}{4}$, 12$\frac{1}{2}$, 13$\frac{1}{4}$, 14, 15)" / 28 (30, 32, 34, 36, 38) cm, K2tog at this edge every 3rd row 27 times.

Shape armholes

Row 1 Bind / cast off 6 sts, cont in patt to end.
Row 2 and every even row Work in patt.
Row 3 Bind / cast off 3 (3, 4, 5, 5, 5) sts, cont in patt to end.
Row 5 Bind / cast off 2 (2, 2, 3, 4, 4) sts, cont in patt to end.
Row 7 Bind / cast off 1 (1, 1, 2, 2, 3) sts, cont in patt to end.
Row 9 Bind / cast off 1 (1, 1, 2, 2, 2) sts, cont in patt to end.
Row 11 Bind / cast off 1 (1, 1, 1, 1, 2) sts, cont in patt to end.
Row 13 Bind / cast off 0 (1, 1, 1, 1, 1) sts, cont in patt to end.
Row 15 Bind / cast off 0 (0, 1, 0, 1, 1) sts, cont in patt to end [24 (24, 24, 25, 26, 26) sts].

Cont even / straight till Front meas 21 (21$\frac{1}{2}$, 22$\frac{3}{4}$, 23$\frac{1}{2}$, 24$\frac{3}{4}$, 25$\frac{1}{2}$)" / 53 (55, 58, 60, 63, 65) cm.

Shape shoulders

Row 1 Bind / cast off 6 (6, 6, 7, 7, 7) sts, cont in patt to end.
Row 2 and every even row Work in patt.
Row 3 Bind / cast off 6 (6, 6, 6, 7, 7) sts, cont in patt to end.
Row 5 Bind / cast off 6 sts, cont in patt to end.
Row 7 Bind / cast off the rem 6 sts. **

RIGHT FRONT

With size 5 US / 3.75mm needles and Indigo yarn cast on 65 (66, 68, 72, 75, 77) sts and work even / straight in patt for 2" / 5 cm.

K2tog at beg of next row (WS) and every 4th row 8 times, to shape side edge. **At the same time**, when work meas 3 (3¼, 3½, 3¾, 4, 4¼)" / 7.5 (8, 9, 9.5, 10, 11) cm make a buttonhole as follows:

Next row (RS) Work 4 sts in patt, bind / cast off 5, work in patt to end of row.

Next row Work in patt casting on 5 sts where they were bound / cast off in the previous row.

When Front meas 4" / 10 cm, insert the pocket as follows:

Next row (WS) P till 51 sts rem, slip the next 31 sts onto a st holder, P to end of row.

Next row Work 20 sts in patt, work the 31 sts from the second pocket, cont in patt to end of row.

Now rep from ** to ** in instructions for Left Front. Rev the shapings, but make 2 more buttonholes at front edge, 3 (3¼, 3½, 3¾, 4, 4¼)" / 7½ (8, 9, 9½, 10, 11) cm apart.

Cardigan with Contrasting Collar

SLEEVES (both alike)

With size 3 US / 3.25mm needles and Indigo yarn cast on 50 (52, 54, 58, 60, 62) sts and work in rib of K1, P1, for 2½" / 6 cm.

Change to size 5 US / 3.75mm needles and work in patt. Inc 1 st at beg and end of 5th row and then every 6th row till there are 86 (88, 92, 92, 94, 96) sts on needle.

Cont even / straight in patt till sleeve meas 17¾ (17¾, 18, 18, 18, 18½)" / 45 (45, 46, 46, 46, 47) cm.

Shape top

Bind / cast off 6 sts at beg of next 2 rows.

Bind / cast off 3 sts at beg of next 2 rows.

Bind / cast off 2 sts at beg of next 2 rows.

K2tog at beg and end of next and every alt row till there are 28 (28, 30, 30, 32, 32) sts left on needle.

Bind / cast off.

COMBINED COLLAR AND LAPELS

These are worked in st st. Make 2 the same, one in Indigo, one in White.

With size 5 US / 3.75mm needles cast on 20 sts and work 1 row.

Cast on 6 sts at beg of every row for 18 rows (128 sts).

Work 11 rows in st st, ending with a P row.

Next row K54, bind / cast off 20, K54.

Next row P54, join on another ball of same yarn at last 54 sts and P54.

Cont work on both sections (but using 2 balls of yarn), K2tog at the inside edge of both sections every row till 42 sts rem each side.

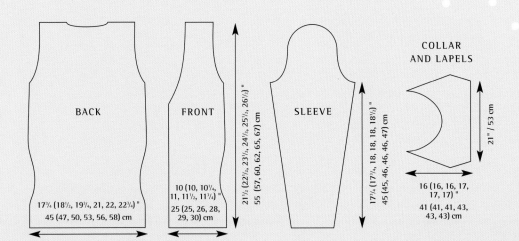

BACK

17¾ (18½, 19¾, 21, 22, 22¾) "
45 (47, 50, 53, 56, 58) cm

FRONT

10 (10, 10¼, 11, 11½, 11¾) "
25 (25, 26, 28, 29, 30) cm

21½ (22¼, 23¾, 24½, 25½, 26½) "
55 (57, 60, 62, 65, 67) cm

SLEEVE

17¾ (17¾, 18, 18, 18, 18½) "
45 (45, 46, 46, 46, 47) cm

COLLAR AND LAPELS

21" / 53 cm

16 (16, 16, 17, 17, 17) "
41 (41, 41, 43, 43, 43) cm

POCKET TOPS (both alike)

Slip the sts on the st holder at the top of the pocket onto a size 3 US / 3.25mm needle.

Join on Indigo yarn and work in rib of K1, P1 for 1" / 2.5 cm.

Bind / cast off.

FINISHING

Press and join all seams.

Turn in 2 rows all along bottom part of cardigan and 1 st up along Left and Right Front till dec for collar and stitch down.

With right sides facing, stitch the 2 Collar pieces together at outer edges. Turn to right side and sew both inside edges to neck edge of cardigan with the points of the Collar attached to start of dec on Fronts.

Fold Collar back as shown to give lapel and collar effect and sew one small button to each side.

Sew larger buttons onto the Left Front.

Sew in the pocket lining.

K2tog at the inner edges every alt row till 38 sts rem each side.

K2tog at the outer edges every 4th row, and **at the same time** K2tog at the inner edges every 10th (10th, 10th, 12th, 12th, 12th) row, till 17 sts rem each side.

K2tog at the outer edges every alt row till 9 sts rem each side.

K2tog at the outer edges every row till 4 sts rem each side.

Next row K2tog twice each side.

Bind / cast off.

6 *Tube Top and Bolero*

Make an entrance with this daring modern duo!

FINISHED MEASUREMENTS

To fit bust 32 (34, 36, 38, 40, 42)" / 81 (86, 91, 97, 102, 107) cm

Bolero length 30³⁄₄ (31¹⁄₂, 32¹⁄₄, 33, 34, 34¹⁄₂)" / 78 (80, 82, 84, 86, 88) cm

Bolero width 14¹⁄₂ (15, 15¹⁄₂, 15³⁄₄, 16¹⁄₂, 17)" / 36 (38, 39, 40, 42, 43) cm

Tube Top finished length 13¹⁄₂ (14¹⁄₄, 15, 15³⁄₄, 16¹⁄₂, 17¹⁄₄)" / 34 (36, 38, 40, 42, 44) cm

MATERIALS

Bolero 5 (5, 6, 6, 7, 7) 50 g balls of Jaeger, Aqua in 330 Daffodil

Tube Top 6 (6, 7, 7, 8, 8) 50g balls of Jaeger, Aqua in 330 Daffodil

1 pair size 1 US / 2.25mm needles

1 pair size 2 US / 2.75mm needles

Elastic for Tube Top 1" wide, 48" long / 2 cm wide, 120 cm long

GAUGE / TENSION

Lightly pressed, 30 sts and 30 rows = 4" / 10 cm in pattern using size 2 US / 2.75mm needles.

PATTERN

Row 1 * K2, P1, rep from * to last st, P1.
Row 2 K1, * K1, P2, rep from * to end.
Row 3 * K into back of 2nd st, K first st, sl both sts off left needle, P1, rep from * to last st, P1.

Rep rows 2 and 3.

Apart from the cuffs on the Bolero, both Tube Top and Bolero are worked entirely in this pattern.

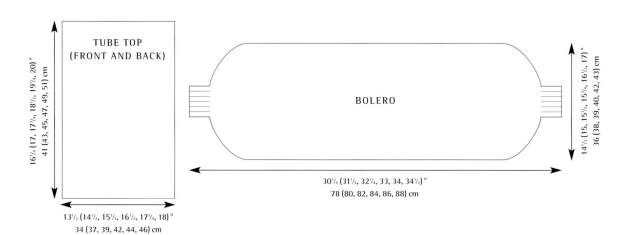

TUBE TOP
(FRONT AND BACK)

16¹⁄₄ (17, 17³⁄₄, 18¹⁄₂, 19¹⁄₄, 20) " / 41 (43, 45, 47, 49, 51) cm

13¹⁄₂ (14¹⁄₂, 15¹⁄₂, 16¹⁄₂, 17¹⁄₄, 18) " / 34 (37, 39, 42, 44, 46) cm

BOLERO

14¹⁄₂ (15, 15¹⁄₄, 15³⁄₄, 16¹⁄₂, 17) " / 36 (38, 39, 40, 42, 43) cm

30¹⁄₄ (31¹⁄₂, 32¹⁄₄, 33, 34, 34¹⁄₂) " / 78 (80, 82, 84, 86, 88) cm

Tube Top and Bolero

BOLERO

With size 1 US / 2.25mm needles cast on 72 (76, 78, 80, 84, 86) sts and work cuff in twisted rib of K-b1, P1 for 2" / 5 cm.

Next row (WS) Cont in K1, P1 rib, inc in every K st till 1 st rem, M1, P1 [109 (115, 118, 121, 127, 130) sts].

Next row (RS) Change to size 2 US / 2.75mm needles and work even / straight in patt till Bolero meas 28¾ (29½, 30¼, 31, 32, 32¾)" / 73 (75, 77, 79, 81, 83) cm from cast on.

Next row (WS) Change to size 1 US / 2.25mm needles and K1, P1 rib, dec by working every 2nd and 3rd sts tog till 2 sts rem, P2tog [72 (76, 78, 80, 84, 86) sts].

Work 2" / 5 cm in twisted rib to create second cuff.

Bind / cast off.

FINISHING

Press lightly on wrong side with damp cloth and warm iron.

Sew up each rib cuff and 2" / 5 cm above. End off firmly on each end.

TUBE TOP

FRONT AND BACK (both alike)

With size 1 US / 2.25mm needles cast on 103 (112, 118, 127, 133, 139) sts and work 12 rows in patt.

Change to size 2 US / 2.75mm needles and work even / straight till Back meas 12¼ (13, 13¾, 14½, 15½, 16¼)" / 31 (33, 35, 37, 39, 41) cm, ending with a RS row.

Change to size 1 US / 2.25mm needles and work 8 rows in patt, ending with a RS row.

Next row (RS of foldover) Change to size 2 US / 2.75mm needles, K1, * P1, K into back of 2nd st, K first st, sl both sts off left needle, rep from * to end.

Next row (WS of foldover) * P2, K1, rep from * to last st, P1.

Rep the last 2 rows till 20 rows have been worked on the foldover.

Bind / cast off.

FINISHING

Sew side seams.

Fold over top and join elastic into circle of 29½ (31½, 33½, 36, 37¾, 39¾)" / 75 (80, 85, 91, 96, 101) cm.

Place elastic on inside of last band of 8 rows worked on size 1 US / 2.25mm needles and stitch in place with herringbone stitch.

Press lightly on wrong side with damp cloth and warm iron.

1951

7 ✕ *Winter Checkmate* 🧶🧶

This sweater is superb good taste – so young, so classic, so sporting!

Row 3   Change to Red. K2, * sl 1 keeping yarn at back, K2, rep from * to end.
Row 4   With Red P2, * sl 1 tbl keeping yarn at front, P2, rep from * to end.

The entire Sweater is worked in this pattern, apart from the ribbing, cuffs and Collar.

FINISHED MEASUREMENTS

To fit bust 32 (34, 36, 38, 40, 42)" / 81 (86, 91, 97, 102, 107) cm

Length 22½ (23¼, 24½, 25¼, 26½, 26¾)" / 57 (59, 62, 64, 67, 68) cm

Sleeve seam length 17¾ (17¾, 18, 18, 18, 18½)" / 45 (45, 46, 46, 46, 47) cm

MATERIALS

9 (10, 10, 11, 12, 13) 50g balls of Debbie Bliss, Rialto in 003 Black

4 (5, 5, 6, 6, 7) 50g balls of Debbie Bliss, Rialto in 012 Red

1 pair size 5 US / 3.75mm needles

1 pair size 7 US / 4.5mm needles

Circular needle size 5 US, 24" long / 3.75mm, 60 cm long

GAUGE / TENSION

24 sts and 34 rows = 4" / 10 cm in pattern using size 7 US / 4.5mm needles

PATTERN

Row 1   K in Black.
Row 2   P in Black.

1957

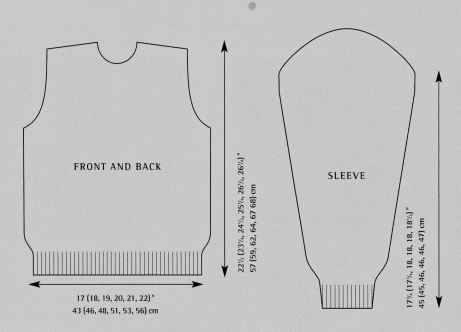

FRONT AND BACK

22½ (23¼, 24½, 25¼, 26½, 26¾)"
57 (59, 62, 64, 67 68) cm

17 (18, 19, 20, 21, 22) "
43 (46, 48, 51, 53, 56) cm

SLEEVE

17¼ (17¼, 18, 18, 18, 18½)"
45 (45, 46, 46, 46, 47) cm

BACK

With size 5 US / 3.75mm needles and Black cast on 104 (108, 116, 120, 128, 132) sts and work 3" / 7.5 cm in K2, P2 rib.

On last row of rib inc 1 st at beg and end for 2nd, 4th and 6th size so there are 104 (110, 116, 122, 128, 134) sts on needle.

Change to size 7 US / 4.5mm needles.

Work even / straight in patt till Back meas 15¾ (16½, 17¼, 18, 19, 19¼)" / 40 (42, 44, 46, 48, 49) cm.

Shape armholes

Bind / cast off 12 (12, 15, 15, 18, 18) sts at beg of next 2 rows.

Cont even / straight on rem 80 (86, 86, 92, 92, 98) sts till Back meas 21½ (22½, 23½, 24½, 25½, 26)" / 55 (57, 60, 62, 65, 66) cm.

Shape shoulders

Bind / cast off 9 (9, 9, 10, 10, 10) sts at beg of next 6 rows.

Bind / cast off rem 26 (32, 32, 32, 32, 38) sts.

FRONT

Work as for Back till armhole shaping is completed.

Cont even / straight till Front meas 19¼ (20, 21¼, 22, 23¼, 23½)" / 49 (51, 54, 56, 59, 60) cm, ending after patt Row 1.

Shape neck

Next row (WS) P33 (36, 36, 39, 39, 42) sts, bind / cast off 14 sts, P to end.

Cont on second set of sts and dec 1 st at neck edge on every row till 27 (27, 27, 30, 30, 30) sts rem.

Cont even / straight till Front meas 21½ {22½, 23½, 24½, 25½, 26)" / 55 (57, 60, 62, 65, 66) cm, ending with a WS row.

Shape shoulder

Bind / cast off 9 (9, 9, 10, 10, 10) sts at beg of next row and foll alt rows.

With RS facing join yarn to neck edge of rem sts and complete this side to match first.

SLEEVES (both alike)

With size 5 US / 3.75mm needles cast on 40 (44, 44, 48, 48, 52) sts and work 3" / 7.5 cm in K2, P2 rib.

On last row of rib inc 1 st at beg of row for 1st and 6th size and at beg and end of row for 4th and 5th size so there are 41 (44, 44, 50, 50, 53) sts on needle.

Change to size 7 US / 4.5mm needles.

Work in patt and inc 1 st at beg and end of every 6th row till there are 77 (80, 84, 88, 92, 95) sts on needle.

Cont even / straight till Sleeve meas 17¾ (17¾, 18, 18, 18, 18½)" / 45 (45, 46, 46, 46, 47) cm.

Place markers of contrasting yarn at each end to indicate end of sleeve seam.

Work even / straight for 2 (2, 2½, 2½, 3, 3)" / 5 (5, 6, 6, 7.5, 7.5) cm.

Shape top

Bind / cast off 6 sts at beg of next 10 rows.

Bind / cast off the rem 17 (20, 24, 28, 32, 35) sts.

Sew shoulder seams.

COLLAR

With Black yarn and circular needle pick up and knit 72 (72, 80, 80, 88, 88) sts all around neck.

Round 1 K twice into every st [144 (144, 160, 160, 176, 176) sts].

Working in rounds, cont even / straight in K2, P2 rib till Collar meas 10" / 25 cm.

Bind / cast off in rib.

FINISHING

Press work lightly on wrong side, avoiding ribbing.

Sew in sleeves, joining last 2 (2, 2½, 2½, 3, 3)" / 5 (5, 6, 6, 7.5, 7.5) cm above markers to bind / cast off edges of armhole shapings.

Join side and sleeve seams.

33

8 | *Evening Wrap*

The chic of simplicity: this wrap will enhance any evening gown.

FINISHED MEASUREMENTS

To fit bust 32 (34, 36, 38, 40, 42)" / 81 (86, 91, 97, 102, 107) cm

MATERIALS

10 (10, 11, 11, 12, 12) 50g balls of Jaeger, Extra Fine Merino DK in 991 Logan Berry

1 pair size 5 US / 3.25mm needles

GAUGE / TENSION

24 sts and 62 rows = 4" / 10 cm in pattern using size 5 US / 3.25mm needles

To measure length accurately, lay work flat and allow 'ribs' to close.

PATTERN

Row 1 K.
Row 2 P.
Row 3 K.
Row 4 K.
Row 5 P.
Row 6 K.

The entire Wrap is worked in this pattern.

WRAP

Cast on 80 sts.

Work even / straight in patt till work meas 11 (12, 13, 14, 15, 16)" / 28 (30.5, 33, 35.5, 38, 40.5) cm.

Next row Cast on 80 sts at beg of row and work across all 160 sts.

Work even / straight till wide part of work meas 14¼ (14¼, 14½, 14½, 15, 15)" / 36 (36, 37, 37, 38, 38) cm.

Next row Bind / cast off 80 sts at beg of row (on same edge as the 80 sts previously cast on).

Work even / straight for a further 11 (12, 13, 14, 15, 16)" / 28 (30.5, 33, 35.5, 38, 40.5) cm.

Bind / cast off.

FINISHING

Lay flat. Fold in centre piece formed by the extra 80 sts.

Fold over each end as illustrated and stitch end of work to each side of centre piece, thus forming armholes.

Do not press.

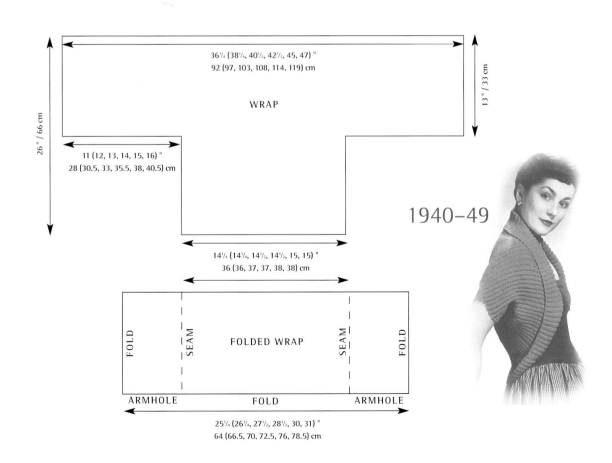

36¼ (38¼, 40½, 42½, 45, 47) "
92 (97, 103, 108, 114, 119) cm

WRAP

13 " / 33 cm

26 " / 66 cm

11 (12, 13, 14, 15, 16) "
28 (30.5, 33, 35.5, 38, 40.5) cm

14¼ (14¼, 14½, 14½, 15, 15) "
36 (36, 37, 37, 38, 38) cm

1940–49

FOLD   SEAM   FOLDED WRAP   SEAM   FOLD

ARMHOLE   FOLD   ARMHOLE

25¼ (26¼, 27½, 28½, 30, 31) "
64 (66.5, 70, 72.5, 76, 78.5) cm

9 *Silky Twinset: Cardigan*

Lunch with the girls?
Add a slender belt to
complete the look of
this stylish matching set!

FINISHED MEASUREMENTS

To fit bust 32 (34, 36, 38, 40, 42)" / 81 (86, 91, 97, 102, 107) cm

Length 22½ (23¼, 24½, 25¼, 26½, 26¾)" / 57 (59, 62, 64, 67, 68) cm

Sleeve seam length 17¾ (17¾, 18, 18, 18, 18½)" / 45 (45, 46, 46, 46, 47) cm

MATERIALS

11 (11, 12, 12, 13, 13) 50g balls of Twilleys, Silky in 105 Coffee.

1 pair size 1 US / 2.25mm needles

1 pair size 2 US / 2.75mm needles

3 stitch holders

2 buttons

GAUGE / TENSION

36 sts and 45 rows = 4" / 10 cm in pattern using size 2 US / 2.75mm needles

PATTERN FOR CARDIGAN AND SWEATER

Row 1 (RS) P1, K2, * P2, K2, rep from * till 1 st rem, P1.

Row 2 K1, P2, * K2, P2, rep from * till 1 st rem, K1.

Rows 3 and 4 P1, K2, * P2, K2, rep from * till 1 st rem, P1.

BACK

With size 2 US / 2.75mm needles cast on 172 (180, 188, 196, 208, 216) sts and work even / straight in patt till Back meas 15¾ (16½, 17¼, 18, 19, 19¼)" / 40 (42, 44, 46, 48, 49) cm.

Shape armholes

Cont in patt and bind / cast off 5 (5, 6, 6, 7, 7) sts at beg of next 2 rows.

Bind / cast off 4 (4, 5, 5, 6, 6) sts at beg of next 2 rows.

Bind / cast off 3 (3, 4, 4, 4, 5) sts at beg of next 2 rows.

Bind / cast off 2 (2, 3, 3, 3, 4) sts at beg of next 2 rows.

Bind / cast off 1 (2, 2, 2, 2, 3) sts at beg of next 2 rows.

Bind / cast off 1 (1, 1, 1, 2, 2) sts at beg of next 2 rows.

Bind / cast off 1 st at beg of next 8 (10, 6, 10, 12, 10) rows [132 (136, 140, 144, 148, 152) sts].

Cont even / straight in patt till Back meas 21½ (22½, 23½, 24½, 25½, 26)" / 55 (57, 60, 62, 65, 66) cm.

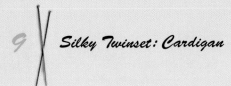

Shape shoulders

Cont in patt and bind / cast off 8 (9, 9, 9, 9, 10) sts at beg of next 2 rows.

Bind / cast off 8 (8, 9, 9, 9, 9) sts at beg of next 2 rows.

Bind / cast off 8 (8, 8, 9, 9, 9) sts at beg of next 2 rows.

Bind / cast off 8 (8, 8, 8, 9, 9) sts at beg of next 2 rows.

Bind / cast off the rem 68 (70, 72, 74, 76, 78) sts.

POCKET LINING (make 2)

With size 2 US / 2.75mm needles cast on 36 sts and work even / straight in patt for 28 rows.

Place sts on st holder.

LEFT FRONT

With size 2 US / 2.75mm needles cast on 92 (96, 100, 104, 108, 112) sts.

Row 1 (RS) Work in patt till 11 sts rem, K11.

Row 2 K11, work in patt to end.

Cont even / straight in patt working a border of 11 g-sts up front edge till 32 rows have been worked.

Next row (RS) Work 21 (25, 29, 33, 37, 41) sts in patt, sl 36 sts onto st holder, work the 36 pocket lining sts in place of these, work 24 sts in patt, K11.

Work even / straight till Front meas 6¼ (6¾, 7¼, 7½, 8, 8)" / 16 (17, 18, 19, 20, 20) cm then dec at front edge as follows:

Next row (RS) Work in patt till 12 sts rem, K2tog, K10.

Work 5 rows in patt, keeping the K11 border at the front edge all the way to top.

Dec like this on every 6th row, taking care to keep patt next to the front border correct as this is very plainly seen on the finished garment.

At the same time, when Front meas 15¾ (16½, 17¼, 18, 19, 19¼)" / 40 (42, 44, 46, 48, 49) cm, shape armhole as follows:

Shape armhole

Row 1 (RS) Bind / cast off 5 (5, 6, 6, 7, 7) sts, cont in patt to end.
Row 2 and every even row Work in patt.
Row 3 Bind / cast off 4 (4, 5, 5, 6, 6) sts, cont in patt to end.
Row 5 Bind / cast off 3 (3, 4, 4, 4, 5) sts, cont in patt to end.
Row 7 Bind / cast off 2 (2, 3, 3, 3, 4) sts, cont in patt to end.
Row 9 Bind / cast off 1 (2, 2, 2, 2, 3) sts, cont in patt to end.

1930–39

Row 10 Bind / cast off 1 (1, 1, 1, 2, 2) sts, cont in patt to end.

Dec 1 st at beg of alt rows (armhole end) 4 (5, 3, 5, 6, 5) times.

Work even / straight at the arm end, but cont the front dec till 43 (44, 45, 46, 47, 48) sts rem.

Cont even / straight in patt till Back meas 21½ (22½, 23½, 24½, 25½, 26)" / 55 (57, 60, 62, 65, 66) cm.

Shape shoulder

Row 1 Bind / cast off 8 (9, 9, 9, 9, 10) sts, cont in patt to end.
Row 2 and every even row Work in patt.
Row 3 Bind / cast off 8 (8, 9, 9, 9, 9) sts, cont in patt to end.
Row 5 Bind / cast off 8 (8, 8, 9, 9, 9) sts, cont in patt to end.
Row 7 Bind / cast off 8 (8, 8, 8, 9, 9) sts [11 sts].

With size 1 US / 2.25mm needles K24 (25, 26, 27, 28, 29) rows on these 11 sts for half of the back neckband.

Bind / cast off.

RIGHT FRONT

With size 2 US / 2.75mm needles cast on 92 (96, 100, 104, 108, 112) sts.

Row 1 (RS) K11 for the front border, * P2, K2, rep from * till 1 st rem, P1.
Row 2 K1, * P2, K2, rep from * till 11 sts rem, K11.
Row 3 As row 1.
Row 4 P1, * K2, P2, rep from * till 11 sts rem, K11.

Rep these 4 rows and work as for Left Front, but rev the shapings.

RIGHT SLEEVE

Right part of wristband With size 1 US / 2.25mm needles cast on 32 (34, 36, 38, 40, 42) sts and work 16 rows in g-st. Place on st holder.

Left part of wristband With size 1 US / 2.25mm needles cast on 48 (50, 52, 54, 56, 58) sts and work 7 rows in g-st.

Next row K6, bind / cast off 4 sts, K38 (40, 42, 44, 46, 48).

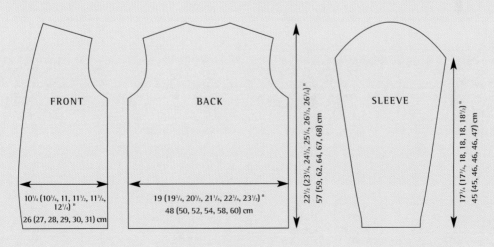

FRONT

10¼ (10¼, 11, 11½, 11¾, 12¼) "
26 (27, 28, 29, 30, 31) cm

BACK

19 (19¾, 20½, 21¼, 22¾, 23½) "
48 (50, 52, 54, 58, 60) cm

22½ (23¼, 24¼, 25¼, 26½, 26¾) "
57 (59, 62, 64, 67, 68) cm

SLEEVE

17¼ (17¾, 18, 18, 18, 18½) "
45 (45, 46, 46, 46, 47) cm

Next row K38 (40, 42, 44, 46, 48), cast on 4 sts over those bound / cast off on previous row, K6.

Work 7 rows in g-st.

Next row (RS) Change to size 2 US / 2.75mm needles and in patt work 36 (38, 40, 42, 44, 46) sts from left wristband, (in patt work 1 st from left wristband tog with 1 st from right wristband) 12 times, work in patt the last 20 (22, 24, 26, 28, 30) sts from right wristband [68 (72, 76, 80, 84, 88) sts].

** Cont in patt and work 10 rows even / straight.

Inc 1 st at beg and end of next and every foll 6th row till there are 124 (128, 132, 136, 140, 144) sts on needle.

Cont even / straight in patt till Sleeve meas 17¾ (17¾, 18, 18, 18, 18½)" / 45 (45, 46, 46, 46, 47) cm.

Shape top

Cont in patt and bind / cast off 5 (5, 6, 6, 7, 7) sts at beg of next 2 rows.

Bind / cast off 4 (4, 5, 5, 6, 6) sts at beg of next 2 rows.

Bind / cast off 3 (3, 4, 4, 4, 5) sts at beg of next 2 rows.

Bind / cast off 2 (2, 3, 3, 3, 4) sts at beg of next 2 rows.

Bind / cast off 1 (2, 2, 2, 2, 3) sts at beg of next 2 rows.

Bind / cast off 1 (1, 1, 1, 2, 2) sts at beg of next 2 rows.

Dec 1 st at beg of next 14 (12, 30, 28, 40, 44) rows

Dec 1 st at beg and end of every row till 22 (24, 26, 28, 30, 32) sts rem.

Bind / cast off.

LEFT SLEEVE

Left part of wristband With size 1 US / 2.25mm needles cast on 32 (34, 36, 38, 40, 42) sts and work 16 rows in g-st. Place on st holder.

Right part of wristband With size 1 US / 2.25mm needles cast on 48 (50, 52, 54, 56, 58) sts and work 7 rows in g-st.

Next row K38 (40, 42, 44, 46, 48), bind / cast off 4 sts, K6.

Next row K6, cast on 4 sts over those bound / cast off on previous row, K38 (40, 42, 44, 46, 48).

Work 7 rows in g-st.

Next row (RS) Change to size 2 US / 2.75mm needles and in patt work 36 (38, 40, 42, 44, 46) sts from left wristband (in patt work 1 st from left wristband tog with 1 st from right wristband) 12 times, work in patt the last 20 (22, 24, 26, 28, 30) sts from right wristband [68 (72, 76, 80, 84, 88) sts].

Cont from ** on Right Sleeve to bind / cast off.

POCKET TOPS

Slip the pocket top 36 sts onto size 1 US / 2.25mm needles and work 7 rows in g-st.

Bind / cast off loosely.

FINISHING

Sew shoulder, side and sleeve seams.

Sew in the sleeves.

Sew front bands together at the neck and sew onto Back.

Sew the sides of the pocket tops down and sew in the pocket linings.

Sew on buttons.

Silky Twinset: Sweater

FINISHED MEASUREMENTS

To fit bust 32 (34, 36, 38, 40, 42)" / 81 (86, 91, 97, 102, 107) cm

Length 22½ (23¼, 24½, 25¼, 26½, 26¾)" / 57 (59, 62, 64, 67, 68) cm

Sleeve seam length 17¾ (17¾, 18, 18, 18, 18½)" / 45 (45, 46, 46, 46, 47) cm

MATERIALS

11 (11, 12, 12, 13, 13) 50g balls of Twilleys, Silky in 105 Coffee.

1 pair size 1 US / 2.25mm needles

1 pair size 2 US / 2.75mm needles

7 buttons

GAUGE / TENSION

36 sts and 45 rows = 4" / 10 cm in pattern using size 2 US / 2.75mm needles

BACK

With size 2 US / 2.75mm needles cast on 172 (180, 188, 196, 208, 216) sts and work even / straight in patt (as for cardigan, see p. 37) till Back meas 15¾ (16½, 17¼, 18, 19, 19¼)" / 40 (42, 44, 46, 48, 49) cm.

Shape armholes

Cont in patt and bind / cast off 5 (5, 6, 6, 7, 7) sts at beg of next 2 rows.

Bind / cast off 4 (4, 5, 5, 6, 6) sts at beg of next 2 rows.

Bind / cast off 3 (3, 4, 4, 4, 5) sts at beg of next 2 rows.

Bind / cast off 2 (2, 3, 3, 3, 4) sts at beg of next 2 rows.

Bind / cast off 1 (2, 2, 2, 2, 3) sts at beg of next 2 rows.

Bind / cast off 1 (1, 1, 1, 2, 2) sts at beg of next 2 rows.

Bind / cast off 1 st at beg of next 8 (10, 6, 10, 12, 10) rows [132 (136, 140, 144, 148, 152) sts].

Cont even / straight in patt till Back meas 21½ (22½, 23½, 24½, 25½, 26)" / 55 (57, 60, 62, 65, 66) cm.

Shape neck and shoulders

Row 1 (WS) Work 32 (33, 34, 35, 36, 37) sts in patt for the left shoulder, bind / cast off 68 (70, 72, 74, 76, 78) sts, work 32 (33, 34, 35, 36, 37) sts in patt for the right shoulder.

Cont to shape right shoulder as follows:
Row 2 Bind / cast off 8 (9, 9, 9, 9, 10) sts, work in patt to end.
Row 3, 5, 7 Work in patt.
Row 4 Bind / cast off 8 (8, 9, 9, 9, 9) sts, work in patt to end.
Row 6 Bind / cast off 8 (8, 8, 9, 9, 9) sts, work in patt to end.
Row 8 Bind / cast off the rem 8 (8, 8, 8, 9, 9) sts.

Join yarn to the neck edge at left shoulder and work 1 row in patt.

Row 2–8 Work as for right shoulder.

LEFT FRONT

With size 2 US / 2.75mm needles cast on 92 (96, 100, 104, 108, 112) sts.

Row 1 (RS) Work in patt till 11 sts rem, K11.
Row 2 K11, work in patt to end.

Cont even / straight in patt working a border of 11 g-sts up front edge till Front meas 15¾ (16½, 17¼, 18, 19, 19¼)" / 40 (42, 44, 46, 48, 49) cm.

Shape armhole

Row 1 (RS) Bind / cast off 5 (5, 6, 6, 7, 7) sts at beg of row. Cont in patt to end, keeping the K11 border at the front edge.
Row 2 and every even row Work in patt.
Row 3 Bind / cast off 4 (4, 5, 5, 6, 6) sts at beg of row.

Row 5 Bind / cast off 3 (3, 4, 4, 4, 5) sts at beg of row.
Row 7 Bind / cast off 2 (2, 3, 3, 3, 4) sts at beg of row.
Row 9 Bind / cast off 1 (2, 2, 2, 2, 3) sts at beg of row.
Row 11 Bind / cast off 1 (1, 1, 1, 2, 2) sts at beg of row.

Dec 1 st at beg of alt rows (armhole end) 4 (5, 3, 5, 6, 5) times.

Cont even / straight in patt till Front meas 19¼ (20, 21¼, 22, 23¼, 23½)" / 49 (51, 54, 56, 59, 60) cm.

Shape neck

Row 1 (WS) Bind / cast off 14 sts, cont in patt to end.
Row 2, 4, 6 Work in patt.
Row 3 Bind / cast off 4 sts, cont in patt to end.

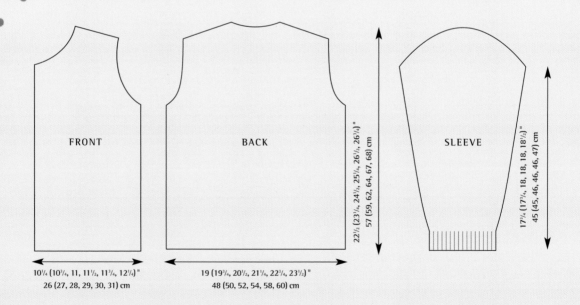

FRONT

10¼ (10¾, 11, 11½, 11¾, 12¼)"
26 (27, 28, 29, 30, 31) cm

BACK

19 (19¾, 20½, 21¼, 22¾, 23½)"
48 (50, 52, 54, 58, 60) cm

22½ (23¼, 24½, 25¼, 26½, 26¾)"
57 (59, 62, 64, 67, 68) cm

SLEEVE

17¼ (17¼, 18, 18, 18, 18½)"
45 (45, 46, 46, 46, 47) cm

Row 5 Bind / cast off 4 sts, cont in patt to end.

Bind / cast off 2 sts at beg of alt rows (neck end) 4 times.

Dec 1 st at beg of alt rows 4 (5, 6, 7, 8, 9) times [32 (33, 34, 35, 36, 37) sts].

Cont even / straight in patt till Front meas 21$\frac{1}{2}$ (22$\frac{1}{2}$, 23$\frac{1}{2}$, 24$\frac{1}{2}$, 25$\frac{1}{2}$, 26)" / 55 (57, 60, 62, 65, 66) cm.

Shape shoulder as for Back.

RIGHT FRONT

With size 2 US / 2.75mm needles cast on 92 (96, 100, 104, 108, 112) sts.

Row 1 (RS) K11 for the front border, * P2, K2, rep from * to last st, P1.
Row 2 K1, * P2, K2, rep from * till 11 sts rem, K11.
Row 3 As row 1.
Row 4 P1, * K2, P2, rep from * till 11 sts rem, K11.

Rep these 4 rows and work as for Left Front, but rev the shapings. **At the same time** when 10 rows have been worked, make the first buttonhole as follows:

Next row (WS) Work in patt till 8 sts rem, bind / cast off 4 sts, K4.

Next row K4, cast on 4 sts over those bound / cast off on previous row, work in patt to end.

Make another 5 buttonholes the same way approximately every 8 (8, 9, 9, 10, 10) cm.

To make the buttonhole distance completely accurate, count the rows on your Left Front till bind / cast off at neck. Then deduct 10 rows (to first buttonhole). Add 6 rows (rows to buttonhole in yoke). Divide the rem rows by 6. This equals the amount of rows to be worked in between each first buttonhole row.

As your very top buttonhole is in the yoke, the top buttonhole on Right Front is approximately 2$\frac{3}{4}$ (2$\frac{3}{4}$, 3$\frac{1}{4}$, 3$\frac{1}{4}$, 3$\frac{1}{2}$, 3$\frac{1}{2}$)" / 7 (7, 8, 8, 9, 9) cm from neck shaping.

Sew shoulder seams.

YOKE

With the right side of the work facing and using size 1 US / 2.25mm needles pick up and knit 133 (133, 157, 157, 181, 181) sts all round the neck.

K 3 rows.

Next row (RS) K12, K2tog, (K10, K2tog) 4 (4, 5, 5, 6, 6) times, K9, K2tog, (K10, K2tog) 4 (4, 5, 5, 6, 6) times, K12 [123 (123, 145, 145, 167, 167) sts].

K 2 rows.

Next row (WS) K till 8 sts rem, bind / cast off 4 sts, K4.

Next row (RS) K4, cast on 4 sts, K4, K2tog, (K9, K2tog) 4 (4, 5, 5, 6, 6) times, K7, K2tog, (K9, K2tog) 4 (4, 5, 5, 6, 6) times, K14 [113 (113, 133, 133, 153, 153) sts].

K 3 rows.

Next row (RS) K11, K2tog, (K8, K2tog) 4 (4, 5, 5, 6, 6) times, K7, K2tog, (K8, K2tog) 4 (4, 5, 5, 6, 6) times, K11 [103 (103, 121, 121, 139, 139) sts].

K 2 rows.

Bind / cast off very loosely.

SLEEVES (both alike)

With size 1 US / 2.25mm needles cast on 56 (60, 64, 68, 72, 76) sts.

Work 26 rows in K2, P2 rib.

Next row (RS) Change to size 2 US / 2.75mm needles and cont in patt inc 1 st at beg and end of next and every 6th row thereafter till there are 112 (116, 120, 124, 128, 132) sts on needle.

Cont even / straight in patt till Sleeve meas 17³/₄ (17³/₄, 18, 18, 18, 18¹/₂)" / 45 (45, 46, 46, 46, 47) cm.

Shape top

Cont in patt and bind / cast off 5 (5, 6, 6, 7, 7) sts at beg of next 2 rows.

Bind / cast off 4 (4, 5, 5, 6, 6) sts at beg of next 2 rows.

Bind / cast off 3 (3, 4, 4, 4, 5) sts at beg of next 2 rows.

Bind / cast off 2 (2, 3, 3, 3, 4) sts at beg of next 2 rows.

Bind / cast off 1 (2, 2, 2, 2, 3) sts at beg of next 2 rows.

Bind / cast off 1 (1, 1, 1, 2, 2) sts at beg ofnext 2 rows.

Dec 1 st at beg of next 6 (28, 44, 42, 50, 52) rows.

Dec 1 st at beg and end of every row till there are 22 (24, 26, 28, 30, 26) sts on needle.

Bind / cast off.

FINISHING

Sew side and sleeve seams.

Sew in sleeves.

Sew on buttons.

10 ✕ Stylish Spring Top

Cast off the weight of winter with this feminine and fashionable sleeveless top.

1958

FINISHED MEASUREMENTS

To fit bust 32 (34, 36, 38, 40, 42)" / 81 (86, 91, 97, 102, 107) cm

Finished length 19¼ (20½, 22, 23¼, 24¾, 26)" / 49 (52, 56, 59, 63, 66) cm

MATERIALS

1 250g cone of Twilleys, Southern Comfort in 83 Spring Green

1 pair size 1 US / 2.25mm needles

1 pair size 2 US / 2.75mm needles

Small amount of polyester stuffing for shoulder straps

Petersham binding 2" wide, 40" long / 5 cm wide, 100 cm long

Elastic 1" wide, 20" long / 2 cm wide, 50 cm long

GAUGE / TENSION

32 sts and 42 rows = 4" / 10 cm in st st using size 2 US / 2.75mm needles

The entire Top is worked in st st.

FRONT AND BACK (both alike)

With size 1 US / 2.25mm needles cast on 130 (138, 146, 156, 164, 172) sts and work 62 rows in st st.

Change to size 2 US / 2.75mm needles and work 2 rows in st st.

Dec 1 st at beg and end of next and every foll 3rd (3rd, 4th, 5th, 6th, 6th) row 11 times [108 (116, 124, 134, 142, 150) sts].

Cont even / straight till Back meas 9 (10, 10¾, 11½, 12¼, 13)" / 23 (25, 27, 29, 31, 33) cm.

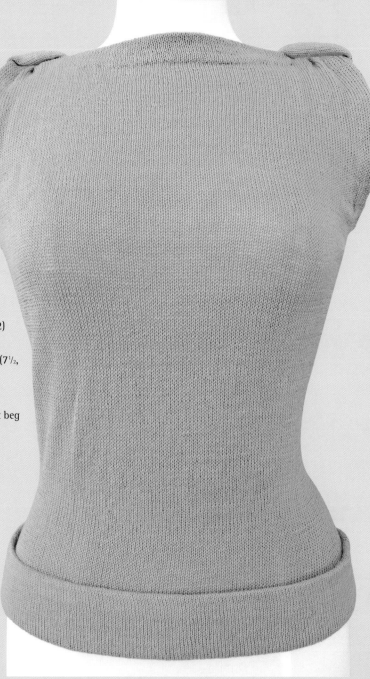

Change to size 1 US / 2.25mm needles and work 16 rows even / straight.

Change to size 2 US / 2.75mm needles and work 4 rows even / straight.

Inc 1 st at beg and end of next and every foll 5th (5th, 6th, 6th, 7th, 7th) row 11 times [130 (138, 146, 156, 164, 172) sts].

Cont even / straight till Back meas 17³/₄ (19, 20, 21¹/₄, 22¹/₂, 23¹/₂)" / 45 (48, 51, 54, 57, 60) cm.

Shape armholes

Bind / cast off 4 sts at beg of next 2 rows.

Dec 1 st at beg and end of next and every foll alt row till 110 (118, 126, 136, 144, 152) sts rem.

Cont even / straight till armholes meas 7¹/₂ (7¹/₂, 8, 8, 8¹/₄, 8¹/₄)" / 19 (19, 20, 20, 21, 21) cm.

Shape shoulders and neck

Bind / cast off 26 (26, 28, 28, 30, 30) sts at beg of next 2 rows.

Work 10 rows even / straight.

Bind / cast off.

Sew shoulder seams.

ARMHOLE FACINGS (both alike)

With RS of work facing and size 1 US / 2.25mm needles, pick up and knit 142 (146, 152, 156, 160, 164) sts around armhole and work 6 rows even / straight.

Bind / cast off.

SHOULDER STRAPS (make 2)

With size 1 US / 2.25mm needles cast on 18 sts.

Work 48 rows even / straight.

Bind / cast off.

FINISHING

Press pieces lightly.

Turn in 10 rows at neck edge of Front and Back and stitch down to inside.

Sew side seams.

Cut petersham into 2 pieces of 14$^{1}/_{2}$ (15$^{3}/_{4}$, 16$^{1}/_{2}$, 17$^{3}/_{4}$, 19, 19$^{3}/_{4}$)" / 37 (40, 42, 45, 48, 50) cm.

Cut 4 pieces of elastic each 2" / 5 cm long.

Join petersham at either end with elastic (top and bottom) and form into a circle of 32 (34 36, 38, 40, 42)" / 81 (86, 91, 97, 102, 107) cm.

Meas 19$^{1}/_{4}$ (20$^{1}/_{2}$, 22, 23$^{1}/_{4}$, 24$^{3}/_{4}$, 26)" / 49 (52, 56, 59, 63, 66) cm down from neck edge and stitch loosely all round with a contrasting thread.

With RS of work facing, place petersham on WS and butt its top edge up to the thread. Pin petersham in place on RS.

Fold bottom part of work over petersham and sew neatly on WS.

Turn the petersham up to form the long fold.

Pull out the contrasting thread (which should be at the bottom of the fold).

Turn armhole facings to inside and stitch down.

Pad shoulder straps with polyester stuffing and fold lengthwise before stitching long edges.

Gather shoulders and stitch shoulder straps into position.

Press all seams.

FRONT AND BACK

25$^{1}/_{4}$ (26$^{1}/_{4}$, 28, 29$^{1}/_{4}$, 30$^{1}/_{4}$, 31$^{1}/_{4}$)"
64 (67, 71, 74, 78, 81) cm

16$^{1}/_{4}$ (17, 18, 19$^{1}/_{4}$, 20, 21$^{1}/_{4}$)"
41 (43, 46, 49, 51, 54) cm

11 Small Jacket

This dainty jacket is a joy to make!

FINISHED MEASUREMENTS

To fit bust 32 (34, 36, 38, 40, 42)" /
81 (86, 91, 97, 102, 107) cm

Length 16¼ (17¼, 18, 19¼, 20,
20½)" / 41 (44, 46, 49, 51, 52) cm

Sleeve seam length 9½ (10, 10¼,
10¾, 11, 11½)" / 24 (25, 26, 27,
28, 29) cm

MATERIALS

3 (4, 4, 5, 5, 6) 100g balls of
Farrlacey Alpacas,100% Alpaca DK
in Black

1 pair size 5 US / 3.75mm needles

1 pair size 8 US / 5mm needles

GAUGE / TENSION

22 sts and 24 rows = 4" / 10 cm in
pattern using size 8 US / 5mm
needles

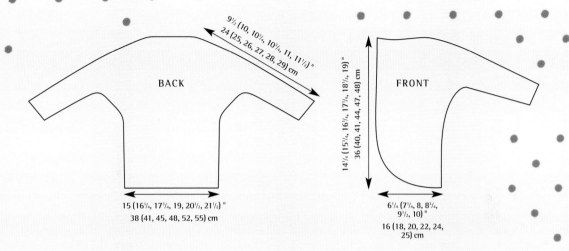

BACK

9½ (10, 10¼, 10¾, 11, 11½)"
24 (25, 26, 27, 28, 29) cm

FRONT

14¼ (15¾, 16¼, 17¼, 18½, 19)"
36 (40, 41, 44, 47, 48) cm

15 (16¼, 17¾, 19, 20½, 21½)"
38 (41, 45, 48, 52, 55) cm

6¼ (7¼, 8, 8¾, 9½, 10)"
16 (18, 20, 22, 24, 25) cm

PATTERN

Row 1 and 3 (RS) * P2, K2, rep from * to last 2 sts, P2.

Row 2 and 4 * K2, P2, rep from * to last 2 sts, K2.

Row 5 * P2, yo / yon, K2 tog tbl, rep from * to last 2 sts, P2.

Row 6 * K2, P2, rep from * to last 2 sts, K2.

The entire Jacket, apart from the bands and lapels, is worked in this pattern.

RIGHT FRONT

With size 8 US / 5mm needles cast on 22 (26, 30, 34, 38, 42) sts.

Working in patt, work 2 rows even / straight and then inc 1 st at front edge of next 8 rows.

Keeping patt correct and front edge even / straight, inc 1 st at side edge on next and every foll 3rd row till there are 36 (40, 44, 48, 52, 56) sts on needle.

Work 2 (4, 6, 8, 10, 12) rows even / straight, then inc 1 st at side edge of foll 4 rows [40 (44, 48, 52, 56, 60) sts].

Cast on 6 sts at side edge of next and every foll alt row twice more [58 (62, 66, 70, 74, 78) sts].

Cast on 10 sts at sleeve edge on next 2 alt rows [78 (82, 86, 90, 94, 98) sts].

Cast on 14 (16, 18, 20, 22, 24) sts at sleeve edge [92 (98, 104, 110, 116, 122) sts].

Keep sleeve edge straight and dec 1 st at front edge on next and every foll 4th row till 84 (89, 94, 99, 104, 110) sts rem, ending at sleeve edge.

Work 2 (2, 0, 0, 2, 0) rows without shaping.

Row 1 Bind / cast off 13 (14, 15, 16, 17, 18) sts at beg of row.

Row 2 and every alt row Work even / straight.

Row 3 Bind / cast off 13 (14, 15, 16, 17, 18) sts, cont in patt to last 3 sts, K2tog, K1.

Row 5 Bind / cast off 9 (10, 11, 12, 13, 14) sts at beg of row.

Row 7 Bind / cast off 9 (10, 11, 12, 13, 14) sts, cont in patt to last 3 sts, K2tog, K1.

Row 9 As row 5.

Row 11 Bind / cast off 7 (7, 7, 7, 7, 8) sts, cont in patt to last 3 sts, K2tog, K1.

Row 13 and 15 Bind / cast off 7 sts at beg of row.

Bind / cast off the rem 7 sts.

LEFT FRONT

Work as for Right Front, but rev the shapings.

BACK

With size 8 US / 5mm needles cast on 70 (78, 86, 94, 102, 110) sts.

Work even / straight in patt for 10 rows and then inc 1 st at beg and end of next and every foll 3rd row till there are 82 (90, 98, 106, 114, 122) sts on needle.

Work 2 (4, 6, 8, 10, 12) rows even / straight, then inc 1 st at beg and end of next 4 rows [90 (98, 106, 114, 122, 130) sts].

Cast on 6 sts at end of next 6 rows [126 (134, 142, 150, 158, 166) sts].

Cast on 10 sts at end of next 4 rows [166 (174, 182, 190, 198, 206) sts].

Cast on 14 (16, 18, 20, 22, 24) sts at end of next 2 rows [194 (206, 218, 230, 242, 254) sts].

Work 30 (34, 36, 42, 46, 46) rows even / straight.

Shape shoulder

Bind / cast off 13 (14, 15, 16, 17, 18) sts at beg of next 4 rows.

Bind / cast off 9 (10, 11, 12, 13, 14) sts at beg of next 6 rows.

Bind / cast off 7 (7, 7, 7, 7, 8) sts at beg of next 2 rows.

Bind / cast off 7 sts at beg of next 6 rows.

Bind / cast off the rem 32 (34, 36, 38, 40, 40) sts.

FRONT BAND AND LAPEL (make 2)

With size 5 US / 3.75mm needles cast on 6 sts and work even / straight in g-st for 1³/₄ (2, 2¹/₄, 2¹/₂, 2³/₄, 3)" / 4 (5, 5.5, 6, 7, 7.5) cm.

Row 1 K to the last 2 sts, inc in the next st, K1.
Row 2 and 3 K.
Row 4 K1, inc in the next st, K to end.
Row 5 and 6 K.

Rep these 6 rows 11 times (30 sts).

Next row Bind / cast off 20 sts, K to end.

Work even / straight in g-st for 13 (13¹/₂, 13³/₄, 14¹/₂, 15, 15¹/₂)" / 33 (34, 35, 37, 38, 39) cm or till band matches length from middle of neck to side seam of Front.

Bind / cast off.

BACK WAISTBAND

With size 5 US / 3.75mm needles cast on 10 sts and work in g-st for 12¹/₂ (13³/₄, 15¹/₂, 17, 18, 19³/₄)" / 32 (35, 39, 43, 46, 50) cm or till band is long enough to fit lower edge of Back.

Bind / cast off.

SLEEVE BANDS (make 2)

With size 5 US / 3.75mm needles cast on 13 sts and work in g-st for 10 (11¹/₂, 12¹/₄, 13³/₄, 15, 15)" / 25 (29, 31, 35, 38, 38) cm or till band is long enough to fit around the lower edge of sleeve.

Bind / cast off.

FINISHING

Press lightly.

Join side and sleeve seams.

Join shoulder seams.

Sew back waistband to lower edge of Back.

Making sure shaped lapels are on same edge of band, join front bands along cast-on edge.

Placing this seam to the centre back of neck, sew on band, placing shaped edge to the front on each side, sewing neatly round the curve and joining

1957

the 10 bound / cast off sts to the ends of the back waistband on each side. Turn back the lapels.

Join sleeve bands and sew to the sleeve edge. Turn back to form a cuff.

Press all seams lightly.

12 / *Leaf-Pattern Sweater*

Perfect for watching sports, days in the country or informal wear.

FINISHED MEASUREMENTS

To fit bust 32 (34, 36, 38, 40, 42)" / 81 (86, 91, 97, 102, 107) cm

Length 20 (20, 21¼, 21¼, 21½, 21½)" / 51 (51, 54, 54, 55, 55) cm

Sleeve seam length 17¾ (17¾, 18, 18, 18, 18½)" / 45 (45, 46, 46, 46, 47) cm

MATERIALS

9 (10, 11, 11, 12, 13) 50g balls of Jaeger Matchmaker Merino DK, 662 Cream

1 pair size 3 US / 3.25mm needles

1 pair size 5 US / 3.75mm needles

1 circular needle size 3 US, 16" long / 3.25mm, 40 cm long

2 stitch holders

GAUGE / TENSION

21 sts and 32 rows = 4" / 10 cm in pattern using size 5 US / 3.75mm needles

PATTERN

Row 1 (RS) P7, * M1, K1, M1, P15, rep from * to last 8 sts, M1, K1, M1, P7.

Row 2 K7, * P3, K15, rep from * to last 10 sts, P3, K7.

Row 3 P7, * M1, K3, M1, P15, rep from * to last 10 sts, M1, K3, M1, P7.

Row 4 K7, * P5, K15, rep from * to last 12 sts, P5, K7.

Row 5 P7, * M1, K1, sl 1, K1, psso, K2, M1, P15, rep from * to last 12 sts, M1, K1, sl 1, K1, psso, K2, M1, P7.

Row 6 K7, * P6, K15, rep from * to last 13 sts, P6, K7.

Row 7 P7, * M1, K2, sl 1, K1, psso, K2, M1, P15, rep from * to last 13 sts, M1, K2, sl 1, K1, psso, K2, M1, P7.

Row 8 K7, * P7, K15, rep from * to last 14 sts, P7, K7.

Row 9 P7, * M1, K3, sl 1, K1, psso, K2, M1, P15, rep from * to last 14 sts, M1, K3, sl 1, K1, psso, K2, M1, P7.

1954

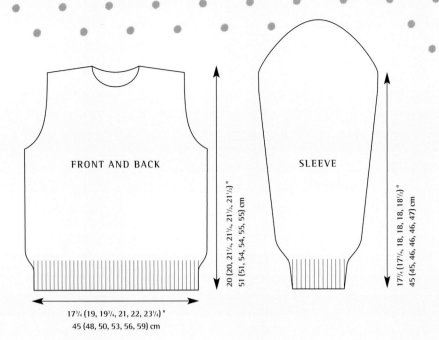

FRONT AND BACK

SLEEVE

17³/₄ (19, 19³/₄, 21, 22, 23¹/₄) "
45 (48, 50, 53, 56, 59) cm

20 (20, 21¹/₄, 21¹/₄, 21¹/₄, 21¹/₂) "
51 (51, 54, 54, 55, 55) cm

17¹/₄ (17¹/₄, 18, 18, 18, 18¹/₂) "
45 (45, 46, 46, 46, 47) cm

Row 10 K7, * P8, K15, rep from * to last 15 sts, P8, K7.

Row 11 P7, * K4, sl 1, K1, psso, K2, P15, rep from * to last 15 sts, K4, sl 1, K1, psso, K2, P7.

Row 12 K7, * P7, K15, rep from * to last 14 sts, P7, K7.

Row 13 P7, * sl 1, K1, psso, K1, sl 1, K1, psso, K2tog, P15, rep from * to last 14 sts, sl 1, K1, psso, K1, sl 1, K1, psso, K2tog, P7.

Row 14 K7, * P4, K15, rep from * to last 11 sts, P4, K7.

Row 15 P7, * sl 1, K1, psso, K2tog, P15, rep from * to last 11 sts, sl 1, K1, psso, K2tog, P7.

Row 16 K7, * P2tog, K15, rep from * to last 9 sts, P2tog, K7.

Row 17 P.

Row 18 K.

Row 19 P.

Row 20 K.

Row 21 * P15, M1, K1, M1, rep from * to last 15 sts, P15.

Row 22 * K15, P3, rep from * to last 15 sts, K15.

Row 23 * P15, M1, K3, M1, rep from * to last 15 sts, P15.

Row 24 * K15, P5, rep from * to last 15 sts, K15.

Row 25 * P15, M1, K1, sl 1, K1, psso, K2, M1, rep from * to last 15 sts, P15.

Row 26 * K15, P6, rep from * to last 15 sts, K15.

Row 27 * P15, M1, K2, sl 1, K1, psso, K2, M1, rep from * to last 15 sts, P15.

Row 28 * K15, P7, rep from * to last 15 sts, K15.

Row 29 * P15, M1, K3, sl 1, K1, psso, K2, M1, rep from * to last 15 sts, P15.

Row 30 * K15, P8, rep from * to last 15 sts, K15.

Row 31 * P15, K4, sl 1, K1, psso, K2, rep from * to last 15 sts, P15.

Row 32 * K15, P7, rep from * to last 15 sts, K15.

Row 33 * P15, sl 1, K1, psso, K1, sl 1, K1, psso, K2tog, rep from * to last 15 sts, P15.

Row 34 * K15, P4, rep from * to last 15 sts, K15.

Row 35 * P15, sl 1, K1, psso, K2tog, rep from * to last 15 sts, P15.

Row 36 * K15, P2tog, rep from * to last 15 sts, K15.

Row 37 P.

Row 38 K.

Row 39 P.

Row 40 K.

These 40 rows form 1 patt.

BACK

With size 3 US / 3.25mm needles cast on 94 (100, 106, 112, 118, 124) sts.

Work 3 (3, 3½, 3½, 4, 4)" / 7½ (7½, 9, 9, 10, 10) cm in K1, P1 rib.

Inc 1 st at end of last rib row [95 (101, 107, 113, 119, 125) sts].

Change to size 5 US / 3.75mm needles.

Next row (RS) P.
Next row K.

Now work in patt keeping 0 (3, 6, 9, 12, 15) extra sts at each end of row in rev st st and working patt over 95 sts.

Work 2 complete patt.

Shape armholes

Bind / cast off 6 (6, 7, 7, 7, 7) sts at beg of next 2 rows.

Bind / cast off 1 (4, 4, 4, 4, 5) sts at beg of next 2 rows.

Bind / cast off 1 (1, 1, 2, 3, 4) sts at beg of next 2 rows.

Bind / cast off 1 (1, 1, 1, 2, 2) sts at beg of next 2 rows.

Dec 1 (0, 1, 1, 1, 1) st at beg of next 2 rows.

Dec 0 (0, 0, 1, 1, 1) st at beg of next 2 rows [75 (77, 79, 81, 83, 85) sts] ✝

Cont even / straight in patt to end of row 16 (16, 18, 18, 20, 20) of 4th patt.

Finish Back in rev st st, as follows:

Shape shoulders

Bind / cast off 8 sts at beg of next 2 rows.

Bind / cast off 8 (8, 8, 9, 9, 9) sts at beg of next 2 rows.

Bind / cast off 9 sts at beg of next 2 rows.

Slip rem 25 (27, 29, 29, 31, 33) sts onto st holder for neck.

FRONT

Follow instructions for Back to †

Cont even / straight in patt to end of row 40 of 3rd patt.

Shape neck

Next row (RS)   P28 (28, 29, 29, 30, 30), turn.

Dec 1 st at this edge every row 3 times [25 (25, 26, 26, 26, 27, 27) sts].

Working leaf at armhole side only, cont even / straight to end of row 16 (16, 16, 18, 18, 18) of 4th patt.

Finish in rev st st, as follows:

Shape shoulders

At armhole edge bind / cast off 8 sts.

At armhole edge bind / cast off 8 (8, 8, 9, 9, 9) sts.

At armhole edge bind / cast off 9 sts.

Slip centre 19 (21, 22, 23, 24, 24) sts onto st holder for neck.

Join yarn to neck edge of rem sts and work as for first side, but rev the shapings.

SLEEVES (both alike)

With size 3 US / 3.25mm needles cast on 46 (48, 50, 52, 54, 56) sts.

Work 3 (3, 3½, 3½, 4, 4)" / 7½ (7½, 9, 9, 10, 10) cm in K1, P1 rib.

Inc 1 st at end of last row [47 (49, 51, 53, 55, 57) sts].

Change to size 5 US / 3.75mm needles and patt, keeping 0 (1, 2, 3, 4, 5) extra sts at each end of row in rev st st and working patt over 47 sts.

Inc 1 st at beg and end of 3rd and every foll 6th row 12 (12, 13, 13, 14, 14) times, working all inc sts into patt [73 (75, 79, 81, 85, 87) sts].

Work to end of row 40 of 3rd patt.

Shape top

Bind / cast off 4 (4, 5, 5, 6, 6) sts at beg of next 2 rows.

Dec 1 st at beg and end of every alt row 14 (13, 15, 14, 16, 15) times. **At the same time** when row 16 (16, 18, 18, 20, 20) of 4th patt has been completed, finish the sleeve in rev st st.

Dec 1 st at beg and end of every row 3 (5, 4, 6, 5, 7) times.

Bind / cast off 3 sts at beg of next 6 rows.

Bind / cast off the rem 13 sts.

NECKBAND

Sew shoulder seams.

With RS of work towards you and circular needle pick up and knit around neck: 25 (27, 29, 29, 31, 33) sts from st holder at back, 26 (26, 28, 28, 30, 30) sts down left side of neck, 19 (21, 22, 23, 24, 24) sts from st holder at front, and 26 (26, 28, 28, 30, 30) sts up right side [96 (100, 107, 108, 115, 117) sts].

Working in rounds of K1, P1 rib, inc 0 (0, 1, 0, 1, 1) sts in first round, and cont even / straight for 3½" / 9 cm.

Bind / cast off loosely in rib.

FINISHING

Sew in sleeves. Sew side and sleeve seams.
Press lightly.

13 / *Angora Leaf Scarf*

This warmer is exceedingly soft, smart and becoming.

FINISHED MEASUREMENTS

Length 34½" / 88 cm

Length of middle section 17¼" / 44 cm

Width of middle section 6¼" / 16 cm

MATERIALS

1 50g Orkney Angora, 100% Angora 4 ply in 26 Natural

3 needles size 3 US / 3.25mm

1 darning needle

1 transparent snap fastener

GAUGE / TENSION

30 sts and 40 rows = 4" / 10 cm in g-st using size 3 US / 3.25mm needles

SCARF

The entire scarf is worked in g-st.

Cast on 3 sts and work in g-st, inc 1 st at beg and end of every alt row till there are 51 sts on needle.

Work 10 rows even / straight.

Dec 1 st at beg and end of every 4th row till there are 29 sts on needle.

Work another leaf in the same way till there are 29 sts on needle.

Next row K20, place the first leaf behind the one you are working on and K tog 1 st from front needle with 1 st from back needle 9 times, K the rem 20 sts [49 sts].

Work 12 rows on these 49 sts.

Next row K24, turn. Work on these 24 sts for 11 rows to create opening.

Return to the 25 sts on other needle and work 11 rows.

On the 12th row work right across the 2 needles [49 sts].

Work 150 rows or length required.

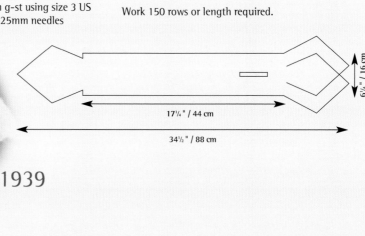

17¼" / 44 cm

34½" / 88 cm

6¼" / 16 cm

1939

Next row K2tog across row till 1 st rem, K1 [25 sts].

Cont in g-st, inc 1 st at beg and end of every 4th row till there are 51 sts on needle.

Work 10 rows even / straight.

Dec 1 st at beg and end of every alt row till 3 sts rem.

Bind / cast off.

FINISHING

With darning needle and double yarn, work in stem-stitch according to diagram to represent veins on each leaf.

Fold scarf into inverted pleat, slip one end through opening and sew on snap fastener to keep scarf in place.

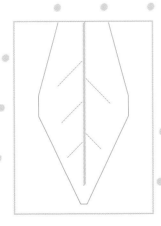

14 Cardigan with First-Class Tailoring

> *Look attractive and trim in this figure-flattering design!*

FINISHED MEASUREMENTS

To fit bust 32 (34, 36, 38, 40, 42)" / 81 (86, 91, 97, 102, 107) cm

Length 20½ (21, 21½, 22, 22¾, 23¼)" / 52 (53, 55, 56, 58, 59) cm

Sleeve seam length 17¾ (17¾, 18, 18, 18, 18½)" / 45 (45, 46, 46, 46, 47) cm

MATERIALS

9 (9, 10, 10, 11, 11) 50g balls of Rowan 4 ply Cotton in 129 Aegean

1 pair size 2 US / 2.75mm needles

1 pair size 3 US / 3.25mm needles

1 circular needle size 2 US, 32" long / 2.75mm, 80 cm long

1 circular needle size 3 US, 32" long / 3.25mm, 80 cm long

5 stitch holders

2 large and 2 small buttons

GAUGE / TENSION

24 sts and 34 rows = 4" / 10 cm in pattern using size 3 US / 3.25mm needles

TUFT

T = Tuft is made from 1 st by working as follows:

K into front of st in the ordinary way, but do not pass st off left-hand needle, (yo / yrn, K1 into the same st) 3 times, then pass st off left-hand needle, making 7 sts in the one.

* Insert left-hand needle into the second st from the point of right-hand needle and draw it over the first st and off the point of the needle, rep from * 5 times more, which completes the Tuft and leaves 1 st.

PATTERN

Row 1 (RS) (and every odd row) K.
Row 2 P.
Row 4 P3, T, * P7, T, rep from * till 3 rem, P3.
Row 6 P.
Row 8 P7, * T, P7, rep from * to end. (The tufts on this row sit exactly between those on last tuft row.)

POCKET LINING (make 2)

With size 3 US / 3.25mm needles cast on 16 sts and work 24 rows in st st.

Slip these sts onto a st holder and cut the yarn.

COAT

With circular needle size 2 US / 2.75mm cast on 212 (224, 236, 248, 260, 272) sts for all round the waist and work back and forth on needle in K2, P2 rib for 10 rows.

1st buttonhole row Rib 4, bind / cast off 6, rib to end.
2nd buttonhole row Rib till 10 sts rem, cast on 6 sts over those bound / cast off on the previous row, rib 4.

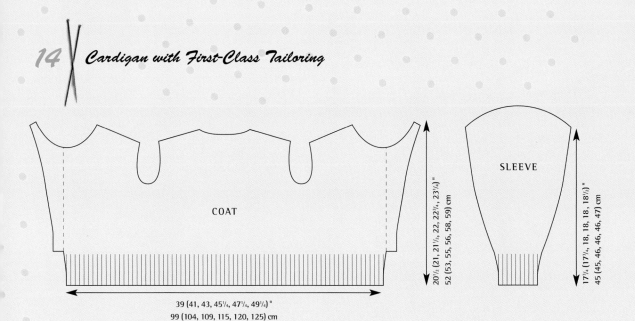

COAT

SLEEVE

39 (41, 43, 45¼, 47¼, 49¼)"
99 (104, 109, 115, 120, 125) cm

20½ (21, 21½, 22, 22¾, 23¾)"
52 (53, 55, 56, 58, 59) cm

17¾ (17¾, 18, 18, 18½)"
45 (45, 46, 46, 46, 47) cm

Work 20 rows in rib.

Rep the 2 buttonhole rows.

Work 9 rows in rib.

Waist inc row (WS) Cast on 12 sts for the left front facing and P these, rib 2 (8, 1, 12, 4, 10), * rib 7 (7, 8, 7, 8, 8), inc in next st, rep from * till 2 (8, 1, 12, 4, 10) sts rem, rib 2 (8, 1, 12, 4, 10), cast on 12 sts for the right front facing [262 (274, 286, 300, 312, 324) sts].

Change to circular needle size 3 US / 3.25mm and cont working back and forth on needle work 8 rows in patt.

Cont in patt till Coat meas 13 (13½, 13¾, 14¼, 14½, 15)" / 33 (34, 35, 36, 37, 38) cm. At the same time inc 1 st for facing at each end of next row and every foll 8th row till 4 rows from very top point.

Next row (RS) K44 (44, 45, 45, 46, 46), slip the next 16 sts onto a st holder for the pocket top, K16 sts from one pocket lining, K150 (162, 173, 187, 198, 210) sts, slip the next 16 sts onto a st holder, K16 sts from last pocket lining, K44

(44, 45, 45, 46, 46) sts [270 (282, 295, 309, 322, 334) sts].

Cont even / straight in patt till work meas 13¾ (14¼, 14½, 15, 15¼, 15¾)" / 35 (36, 37, 38, 39, 40) cm.

Shape armholes

Next row (RS) K80 (83, 86, 89, 93, 95) and slip onto st holder for the Right Front, bind / cast off 6 (6, 7, 8, 8, 10) sts for the first underarm, K98 (104, 109, 115, 120, 124) for the Back and slip sts onto st holder, bind / cast off 6 (6, 7, 8, 8, 10) sts for the second underarm, K80 (83, 86, 89, 93, 95) sts for the Left Front.

LEFT FRONT

Cont in patt. At the revers end inc on every 8th row as before. **At the same time,** shape armhole as follows:

Shape armhole

Row 1 Bind / cast off 2 (3, 3, 3, 3, 3) sts, work in patt till end.

Row 2 and every even row Work in patt.

Row 3 Bind / cast off 2 (2, 2, 3, 3, 3) sts, work in patt till end.

Row 5 Bind / cast off 1 (2, 2, 2, 2, 2) sts, work in patt till end.

Row 7 Bind / cast off 1 (1, 1, 2, 2, 2) sts, work in patt till end.

Row 9 Dec 1 st, work in patt till end.

Row 11 Dec 0 (0, 1, 1, 1, 1) st, work in patt till end.

Row 13 Dec 0 (0, 0, 0, 1, 1) st, work in patt till end.

Row 15 Dec 0 (0, 0, 0, 0, 1) st, work in patt till end.

Cont in patt till Left Front meas 17¾ (18, 18½, 19¼, 20, 20½)" / 45 (46, 47, 49, 51, 52) cm.

Shape neck

Next row (WS) Work 21 (22, 22, 23, 24, 23) sts in patt for the revers facing and slip these sts onto a st holder, bind / cast off 8 (8, 8, 8, 10, 10) sts, patt 48 (49, 50, 51, 52, 53) sts for the Front.

Work in patt, bind / cast off 3 sts at beg of alt rows (neck end) 3 times.

Bind / cast off 2 sts at neck end on alt rows 3 times.

Dec 1 st at neck end on alt rows 3 times. **At the same time** start shaping shoulder as follows:

Shape shoulder

Row 1 (RS) Bind / cast off 9 (9, 9, 9, 9, 10) sts, work in patt till end.

Row 2 and every even row Work in patt.

Row 3 Bind / cast off 8 (8, 8, 8, 9, 9) sts, work in patt till end.

Row 5 Bind / cast off 8 (8, 8, 8, 9, 9) sts, work in patt till end.

Row 7 Bind / cast off the rem 5 (6, 7, 7, 7, 7) sts.

Left front facing

(RS) Join yarn at the neck edge of the facing and work 1 row in patt.

Cont in patt and shape at both ends: at the outside edge inc 1 st on every 8th row as before, at the neck edge bind / cast off 3 sts at the beg of alt rows 3 times.

Bind / cast off 2 sts at neck end on alt rows 3 times.

Dec 1 st at neck end on alt rows 3 times [5 (6, 7, 7, 7, 7) sts].

Work 4 rows even / straight in patt.

Bind / cast off.

BACK

(WS) Join yarn at the left armhole of the Back sts and work 1 row in patt.

Cont in patt, bind / cast off 2 (3, 3, 3, 3, 3) sts at beg of next 2 rows.

Bind / cast off 2 (2, 2, 3, 3, 3) sts at beg of next 2 rows.

Bind / cast off 1 (2, 2, 2, 2, 2) sts at beg of next 2 rows.

Bind / cast off 1 (1, 1, 2, 2, 2) sts at beg of next 2 rows.

Dec 1 st at beg of next 2 (2, 4, 4, 6, 8) rows.

Cont in patt till work meas 19¾ (20, 21, 21¼, 22, 22½)" / 50 (51, 53, 54, 56, 57) cm.

Shape shoulders

Bind / cast off 9 (9, 9, 9, 9, 10) sts at beg of next 2 rows.

Bind / cast off 8 (8, 8, 8, 9, 9) sts at beg of next 2 rows.

Bind / cast off 8 (8, 8, 8, 9, 9) sts at beg of next 2 rows.

Bind / cast off 5 (6, 7, 7, 7, 7) sts at beg of next 2 rows.

Bind / cast off the rem 24 (24, 25, 27, 26, 26) sts.

RIGHT FRONT

(WS) Join yarn at the armhole and work 1 row in patt, then work as for Left Front, rev the shapings.

Right front facing

Join yarn at the neck edge and work 1 row in patt, then work as for left front facing, rev the shapings.

SLEEVES (both alike)

With size 2 US / 2.75mm needles cast on 44 (48, 48, 52, 56, 56) sts and work 44 rows in K2, P2 rib.

Change to size 3 US / 3.25mm needles and work in patt, inc 1 st at beg and end of every 5th row till there are 84 (88, 88, 92, 96, 96) sts on needle.

Cont even / straight in patt till Sleeve meas approximately 17¾ (17¾, 18, 18, 18, 18½)" / 45 (45, 46, 46, 46, 47) cm. The tufts should be in the same position as on the Coat. If necessary, work a couple of rows more to accomplish this.

Shape top

Bind / cast off 6 sts at beg of next 2 rows.

Bind / cast off 3 sts at beg of next 2 rows.

Bind / cast off 2 sts at beg of next 2 rows.

K2tog at beg and end of next and every alt row till there are 28 (28, 30, 30, 32, 32) sts on needle.

Bind / cast off.

POCKET TOPS (both alike)

Slip the pocket top sts onto size 2 US / 2.75mm needles and work 5 rows in K2, P2 rib.

Bind / cast off in rib.

POCKET TABS (make 2)

With size 2 US / 2.75mm needles cast on 12 sts.

K 1 row.

Working in g-st, inc 1 st at beg of next and every alt row till there are 16 sts on needle.

1st buttonhole row (starting at straight end) K7, bind / cast off 5 sts, K4.

2nd buttonhole row K4, cast on 5 sts, K7.

K 1 row.

K2tog at beg of next and every alt row till there are 12 sts on needle.

Bind / cast off.

COLLAR

With size 2 US / 2.75mm needles cast on 130 (130, 134, 134, 138, 138) sts and work 24 rows in K2, P2 rib.

Cont in rib and bind / cast off 20 sts at beg of next 4 rows.

Bind / cast off in rib.

FINISHING

Fold the front facings over to WS and hem lightly.

Join side seams and arm seams, and sew in the sleeves.

Sew the collar on.

Stitch down the pocket tops and sew in the pocket linings.

Sew the pocket tabs onto the main garment.

Sew the buttons on.

OSTRICH

15 | *Light-as-Air Wrap*

Pretty as a picture, this wrap is a garment to cherish.

FINISHED MEASUREMENTS

Length 52 (54, 56, 58, 60, 62)" / 132 (137, 142, 147, 152, 157) cm

Approximate width 30 (30, 30, 39³/₄, 39³/₄, 39³/₄)" / 76 (76, 76, 101, 101, 101) cm

MATERIALS

5 (5, 6, 6, 7, 7) 25g balls of Jamieson & Smith, 2 ply Lace in L1 White

1 pair size 2 US / 2.75mm needles

1 pair size 11 US / 7.5mm needles

1 crochet hook size C US / 3mm

1937

GAUGE / TENSION

It is difficult to measure this pattern, but 15 sts = approx. 4" / 10 cm using size 11 US / 7.5mm needles

PATTERN

Row 1 P.
Row 2 * K19, (K1, yfd, sl 1, yb) 9 times, K1, rep from * to end.
Row 3 * P19, (K1, K P K into next st) 9 times, K1, rep from * to end.
Row 4 * (P1, drop 1 st) 18 times, P1, (K1, yfd, sl 1, yb) 9 times, K1, rep from * to end.

Rep the last 4 rows twice more (12 rows).

Row 13 P.
Row 14 * (K1, yfd, sl 1, yb) 9 times, K1, K19, rep from * to end.
Row 15 * (K1, K P K into next stitch) 9 times, K1, P19, rep from * to end.
Row 16 * (K1, yfd, sl 1, yb) 9 times, K1, (P1, drop 1 st) 18 times, P1, rep from * to end.

Rep the last 4 rows twice more (24 rows).

30 (30, 30, 39³/₄, 39³/₄, 39³/₄)" 76 (76, 76, 101, 101, 101) cm

52 (54, 56, 58, 60, 62)"
132 (137, 142, 147, 152, 157) cm

WRAP

With size 2 US / 2.75mm needles cast on 57 (57, 57, 68, 68, 68) sts.

Work in K1, P1 rib for 6" / 15 cm.

Next row, first 3 sizes K twice into every st (114 sts). There will be this amount of sts after every 4 patt rows.

Next row, last 3 sizes * K twice into each of the first 3 sts and K3 into next st, rep from * till 4 sts rem, K twice into each of the last 4 sts (152 sts). There will be this amount of sts after every 4 patt rows.

Change to size 11 US / 7.5mm needles and work in patt till Wrap meas 46 (48, 50, 52, 54, 56)" / 117 (122, 127, 132, 137, 142) cm from cast on.

Change to size 2 US / 2.75mm needles.

Next row, first 3 sizes K2tog till end [57 sts].

Next row, last 3 sizes * K2tog 3 times, K3tog, rep from * till 8 sts rem, K2tog 4 times [68 sts].

Work in K1, P1 rib for 6" / 15 cm.

Bind / cast off in rib.

FINISHING

Sew the side edges of the ribbing together, to form cuffs.

Work a row of double crochet along the sides of the pattern part.

16 / *Riding Jersey*

A dashing pullover, perfect for teaming with jodhpurs and boots.

PATTERN

Row 1 (RS) K1, * P9, K1, rep from * to end.

Row 2 P1, * K9, P1, rep from * to end.

Row 3 and 4 Rep rows 1 and 2.

Row 5 K1, * K1, P7, K2, rep from * to end.

Row 6 P1, * P1, K7, P2, rep from * to end.

Row 7 and 8 Rep rows 5 and 6.

Row 9 K1, * K2, P5, K3, rep from * to end.

FINISHED MEASUREMENTS

To fit bust 32 (34, 36, 38, 40, 42)" / 81 (86, 91, 97, 102, 107) cm

Length 23¼ (24, 25¼, 26, 27, 27½)" / 59 (61, 64, 66, 69, 70) cm

Sleeve seam length 17¾ (17¾, 18, 18, 18, 18½)" / 45 (45, 46, 46, 46, 47) cm

MATERIALS

5 (6, 6, 7, 7, 8) 100g balls of Farrlacey Alpacas, 100% Alpaca DK in Caramel

1 pair size 3 US / 3.25mm needles

1 pair size 5 US / 3.75mm needles

1 circular needle size 3 US, 24" long / 3.25mm, 60 cm long

1 stitch holder

GAUGE / TENSION

22 sts and 30 rows = 4" / 10 cm in pattern using size 5 US / 3.75mm needles

Row 10 P1, * P2, K5, P3, rep from * to end.
Row 11 and 12 Rep rows 9 and 10.
Row 13 K1, * K3, P3, K4, rep from * to end.
Row 14 P1, * P3, K3, P4, rep from * to end.
Row 15 and 16 Rep rows 13 and 14.
Row 17 K1, * K4, P1, K5, rep from * to end.
Row 18 P1, * P4, K1, P5, rep from * to end.
Row 19 and 20 Rep rows 17 and 18.
Row 21 P1, * K9, P1, rep from * to end.
Row 22 K1, * P9, K1, rep from * to end.
Row 23 and 24 Rep rows 21 and 22.
Row 25 P1, * P1, K7, P2, rep from * to end.
Row 26 K1, * K1, P7, K2, rep from * to end.
Row 27 and 28 Rep rows 25 and 26.
Row 29 P1, * P2, K5, P3, rep from * to end.
Row 30 K1, * K2, P5, K3, rep from * to end.
Row 31 and 32 Rep rows 29 and 30.
Row 33 * P1, P3, K3, P4, rep from * to end.

Row 34 K1, * K3, P3, K4, rep from * to end.
Row 35 and 36 Rep rows 33 and 34.
Row 37 P1, * P4, K1, P5, rep from * to end.
Row 38 K1, * K4, P1, K5, rep from * to end.
Row 39 and 40 Rep rows 37 and 38.

The entire Sweater is worked in this pattern, apart from the rev st st at ribbing, cuffs and neck.

FRONT

With size 5 US / 3.75mm needles cast on 101 (101, 111, 111, 121, 121) sts and work in rev st st for 2" / 5 cm, ending with a K row.

Cont even / straight in patt till Front meas 15³/₄ (16¹/₂, 17¹/₄, 18, 19, 19¹/₄)" / 40 (42, 44, 46, 48, 49) cm.

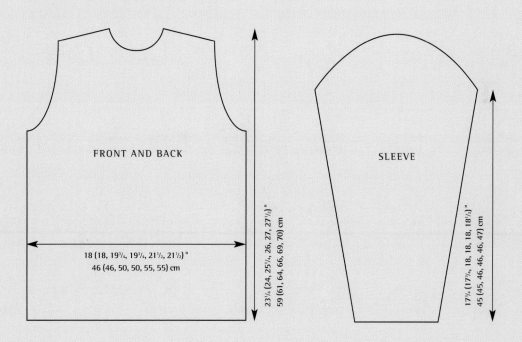

FRONT AND BACK

18 (18, 19³/₄, 19³/₄, 21¹/₂, 21¹/₂) "
46 (46, 50, 50, 55, 55) cm

23¹/₄ (24, 25¹/₄, 26, 27, 27¹/₂)"
59 (61, 64, 66, 69, 70) cm

SLEEVE

17¹/₄ (17¹/₄, 18, 18, 18, 18¹/₂)"
45 (45, 46, 46, 46, 47) cm

Shape armholes

Bind / cast off 5 (5, 6, 6, 6, 6) sts at beg of next 2 rows.

Bind / cast off 3 sts at beg of next 2 rows.

Bind / cast off 2 (2, 2, 2, 3, 3) sts at beg of next 2 rows.

Bind / cast off 1 (1, 2, 2, 2, 2) sts at beg of next 2 rows.

Bind / cast off 1 (1, 1, 1, 2, 2) sts at beg of next 2 rows.

Dec 1 st at beg of next 6 (6, 6, 6, 8, 8) rows [71 (71, 77, 77, 81, 81) sts].

Cont even / straight in patt till Front meas 20³/₄ (21¹/₂, 22³/₄, 23¹/₂, 24³/₄, 25¹/₄)" / 52.5 (54.5, 58, 60, 63, 64) cm.

Shape neck

Next row (RS) Work 32 (32, 34, 34, 36, 36) sts in patt, bind / cast off next 7 (7, 9, 9, 9, 9) sts, cont in patt to end.

Cont in patt on this 2nd set of 32 (32, 34, 34, 36, 36) sts for right side of neck, dec 1 st at neck edge on every row till 18 (18, 20, 20, 22, 22) sts rem.

Shape shoulders

Row 1 (WS) Bind / cast off 6 (6, 7, 7, 8, 8) sts at beg of row.

Row 2 and 4 Work even / straight.

Row 3 Bind / cast off 6 (6, 7, 7, 7, 7) sts at beg of row.

Row 5 Bind / cast off the rem 6 (6, 6, 6, 7, 7) sts.

Rejoin yarn at neck edge to rem 32 (32, 34, 34, 36, 36) sts and work left side to match right.

BACK

Work as for Front till armhole shaping is complete and 71 (71, 77, 77, 81, 81) sts rem.

Cont even / straight till Back meas 22³/₄ (23¹/₂, 24³/₄, 25¹/₂, 26³/₄, 27¹/₄)" / 58 (60, 63, 65, 68, 69) cm.

Shape shoulders

Bind / cast off 6 (6, 7, 7, 8, 8) sts at beg of next 2 rows.

Bind / cast off 6 (6, 7, 7, 7, 7) sts at beg of next 2 rows.

Bind / cast off 6 (6, 6, 6, 7, 7) sts at beg of next 2 rows.

Slip the rem 35 (35, 37, 37, 37, 37) sts onto a st holder.

SLEEVES

With size 3 US / 3.25mm needles cast on 41 (41, 41, 51, 51, 51) sts and work in rev st st for 1" / 2.5 cm ending after a K row.

Change to size 5 US / 3.75mm needles and cont in patt till work meas 2¹/₂" / 5 cm.

Inc 1 st at beg and end of next and every foll 6th row till there are 71 (73, 77, 81, 81, 83) sts on needle.

Cont even / straight in patt till Sleeve meas 17³/₄ (17³/₄, 18, 18, 18, 18¹/₂)" / 45 (45, 46, 46, 46, 47) cm.

Shape top

Bind / cast off 5 (5, 6, 6, 6, 6) sts at beg of next 2 rows.

Bind / cast off 2 sts at beg of next 4 (4, 4, 4, 6, 6) rows.

Dec 1 st at beg and end of next 18 (17, 20, 20, 20, 20) alt rows.

Bind / cast off 2 sts at beg of next 4 (6, 4, 4, 4, 4) rows.

Bind / cast off the rem 9 (9, 9, 13, 9, 11) sts.

Join shoulder seams.

NECK BAND

With RS of work facing and circular needle pick up and knit 80 (80, 84, 84, 84, 84) sts all round neck edge.

Work in rev st st till band meas 1" / 2.5 cm.

Bind / cast off fairly loosely.

FINISHING

Press work lightly.

Join side and sleeve seams and sew in sleeves.

Allow neck band to roll to WS and slip stitch in position.

Turn back and stitch a 1" / 2.5 cm hem at bottom edge and $\frac{1}{2}$" / 1.25 cm hem at cuffs.

Press seams.

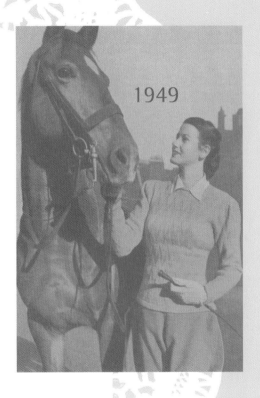

1949

17 Evening Top

> *Off-the-shoulder chic,*
> *superbly slenderizing*
> *in effect!*

FINISHED MEASUREMENTS

To fit bust 32 (34, 36, 38, 40, 42)" / 81 (86, 91, 97, 102, 107) cm

Length from shoulder 17³/₄ (18, 19, 19¹/₄, 20, 20¹/₂) " / 45 (46, 48, 49, 51, 52) cm

MATERIALS

5 (6, 6, 7, 7, 8) 50g balls of Rowan 4 ply Soft in 376 Nippy

1 pair size 2 US / 2.75mm needles

1 pair size 3 US / 3.25mm needles

1 cable needle

Crochet hook size D/3 US / 3.25mm

GAUGE / TENSION

36 sts and 40 rows = 4" / 10 cm in pattern using size 3 US / 3.25mm needles

PATTERN

Row 1 (RS) P3, * K next 2 sts but wind yarn twice round needle for each st instead of once, P4, rep from * to end, but finish last rep with P3 instead of P4.

Row 2 K3, * yfd, sl next 2 sts pw dropping extra loops, yb, K4, rep from * to end, but finish last rep with K3 instead of K4.

Row 3 P3, * sl next 2 sts onto cable needle and leave at front of work, P2, K sts from cable needle tog tbl, P2, rep from * to end but finish last rep with P1 instead of P2.

Row 4 K1, * K twice into next st, K4, rep from * to last st, K1.

Row 5 P1, * K next 2 sts but wind yarn twice round needle for each st instead of once, P4, rep from * to last st, P1.

Row 6 K1, * K4, yfd, sl next 2 sts pw dropping extra loops, yb, rep from * to last st, K1.

Row 7 P1, * sl next 2 sts onto cable needle and leave at front of work, P2, K sts from cable needle tog tbl, P2, rep from * to last st, P1.

Row 8 K1, * K2, K twice into next st, K2, rep from * to last st, K1.

On being Sophisticated

An obvious but unaffected air of quality with a nonchalant acceptance of current fashion lines is essential. The unselfconscious air of quality in Marriner's Heritage wool places it way up top and the latest fashion trends in Marriner leaflet design show the way to sophistication.

Ask to see Marriner leaflet No. 99

In case of difficulty, P.O. 7d., post free from Dept., V.K.

Change to Marriner's

1954

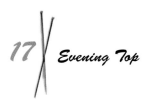

17 Evening Top

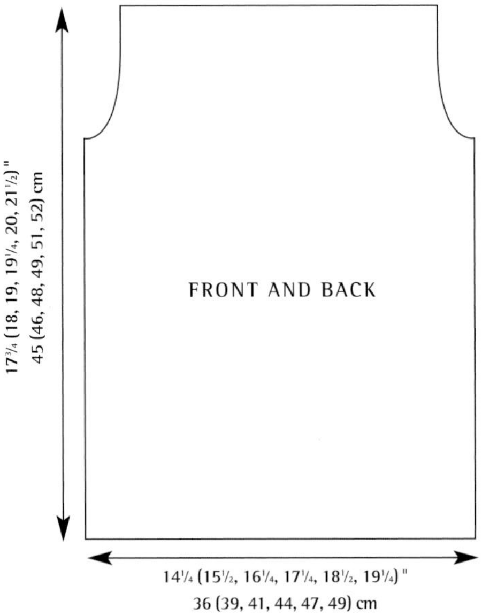
FRONT AND BACK
$17\frac{3}{4}$ (18, 19, $19\frac{1}{4}$, 20, $21\frac{1}{2}$)"
45 (46, 48, 49, 51, 52) cm
$14\frac{1}{4}$ ($15\frac{1}{2}$, $16\frac{1}{4}$, $17\frac{1}{4}$, $18\frac{1}{2}$, $19\frac{1}{4}$)"
36 (39, 41, 44, 47, 49) cm

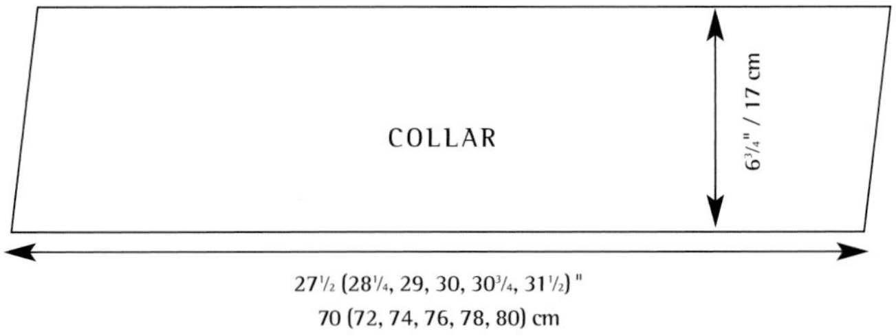
COLLAR
$6\frac{3}{4}$" / 17 cm
$27\frac{1}{2}$ ($28\frac{1}{4}$, 29, 30, $30\frac{3}{4}$, $31\frac{1}{2}$)"
70 (72, 74, 76, 78, 80) cm

FRONT AND BACK (both alike)

With size 2 US / 2.75mm needles cast on 128 (140, 146, 158, 170, 176) sts and K 2 rows.

Cont in patt till work meas $3\frac{1}{2}$" / 9 cm.

Change to size 3 US / 3.25mm needles and cont in patt till work meas $12\frac{1}{2}$ (13, $13\frac{1}{2}$, $13\frac{3}{4}$, $14\frac{1}{4}$, $14\frac{1}{2}$)" / 32 (33, 34, 35, 36, 37) cm.

Shape armholes

Keeping patt correct bind / cast off 5 (5, 5, 7, 7, 7) sts at beg of next 2 rows.

Bind / cast off 2 (3, 3, 4, 4, 4) sts at beg of next 2 rows.

Bind / cast off 2 (2, 2, 2, 2, 3) sts at beg of next 2 rows.

Bind / cast off 1 (1, 1, 2, 2, 2) sts at beg of next 2 rows.

Bind / cast off 1 (1, 1, 1, 1, 2) sts at beg of next 2 rows.

Dec 1 st at beg and end of next and every alt rows 1 (6, 6, 8, 11, 12) times till there are 104 (104, 110, 110, 116, 116) sts on needle.

Work even / straight till work meas $17\frac{3}{4}$ (18, 19, $19\frac{1}{4}$, 20, $20\frac{1}{2}$) " / 45 (46, 48, 49, 51, 52) cm.

Bind / cast off.

COLLAR

With size 3 US / 3.25mm needles cast on 66 sts.

Row 1 K twice into first st, K to last 2 sts, K2tog.
Row 2 P.

Rep these 2 rows till Collar meas $27\frac{1}{2}$ ($28\frac{1}{4}$, 29, 30, $30\frac{3}{4}$, $31\frac{1}{2}$)" / 70 (72, 74, 76, 78, 80) cm along side edge.

Bind / cast off.

FINISHING

This pattern has a tendency to pull to one side, so pin into desired shape and press lightly.

Join side seam.

Join top edges of Front and Back tog for about $1/4$" / 0.5 cm at each side edge.

Work 2 rows of sc / dc around each armhole, drawing edge in slightly to give a good fit.

Join short edges of Collar with a flat seam.

Turn in a $1/2$" / 1 cm hem along one edge of Collar and slip-stitch lightly on WS.

With RS of Collar to WS of work, stitch other edge of Collar all round top of Front and Back, positioning Collar seam in centre of back and easing slightly across shoulders if necessary.

Turn Collar to RS.

Catch the hemmed lower edge in place all along Front, but leave this edge free at Back.

Press seams lightly.

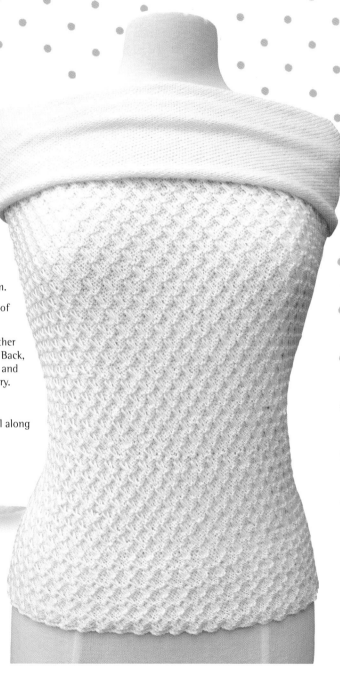

18 | Jacket with Hood

Snug and practical, this is a most up-to-date design.

FINISHED MEASUREMENTS

To fit bust 32 (34, 36, 38, 40, 42)" / 81 (86, 91, 97, 102, 107) cm

Length 21$\frac{1}{2}$ (22$\frac{1}{2}$, 23$\frac{1}{2}$, 24$\frac{1}{2}$, 25$\frac{1}{2}$, 26)" / 55 (57, 60, 62, 65, 66) cm

Sleeve seam length 17$\frac{3}{4}$ (17$\frac{3}{4}$, 18, 18, 18, 18$\frac{1}{2}$)" / 45 (45, 46, 46, 46, 47) cm

MATERIALS

19 (19, 20, 20, 21, 22) 50g balls of RYC, Soft Lux in 001 Pearl

1 pair size 9 US / 5.5mm needles

1 circular needle size 8 US, 32" long / 5mm, 80 cm long

Seven button moulds, diameter 19mm

GAUGE / TENSION

Use double yarn throughout.

14 sts and 22 rows = 4" / 10 cm in pattern using size 9 US / 5.5mm needles

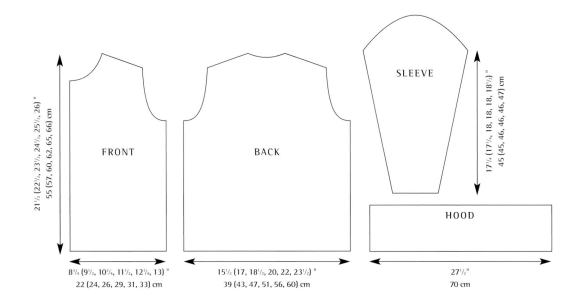

FRONT

8$\frac{1}{4}$ (9$\frac{1}{2}$, 10$\frac{1}{4}$, 11$\frac{1}{2}$, 12$\frac{1}{4}$, 13) "
22 (24, 26, 29, 31, 33) cm

BACK

15$\frac{1}{2}$ (17, 18$\frac{1}{2}$, 20, 22, 23$\frac{1}{2}$) "
39 (43, 47, 51, 56, 60) cm

SLEEVE

HOOD

27$\frac{1}{2}$"
70 cm

21$\frac{1}{2}$ (22$\frac{1}{2}$, 23$\frac{1}{2}$, 24$\frac{1}{2}$, 25$\frac{1}{2}$, 26) "
55 (57, 60, 62, 65, 66) cm

17$\frac{3}{4}$ (17$\frac{3}{4}$, 18, 18, 18, 18$\frac{1}{2}$) "
45 (45, 46, 46, 46, 47) cm

1941

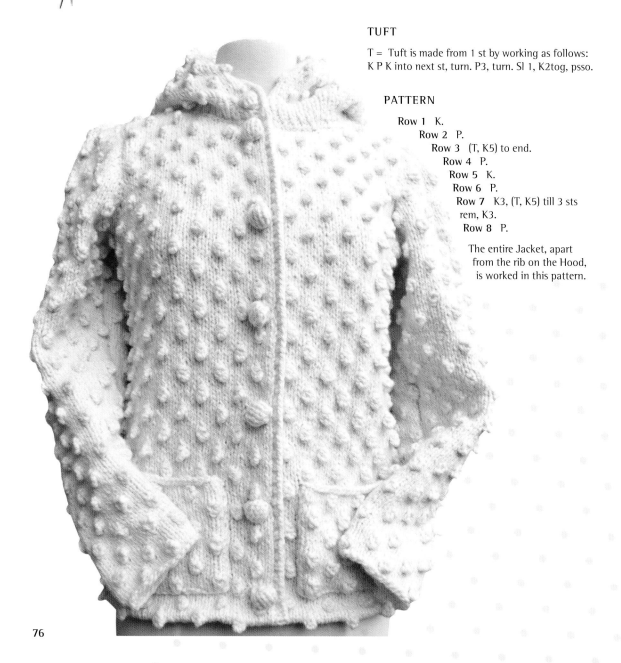

TUFT

T = Tuft is made from 1 st by working as follows: K P K into next st, turn. P3, turn. Sl 1, K2tog, psso.

PATTERN

Row 1   K.

Row 2   P.

Row 3   (T, K5) to end.

Row 4   P.

Row 5   K.

Row 6   P.

Row 7   K3, (T, K5) till 3 sts rem, K3.

Row 8   P.

The entire Jacket, apart from the rib on the Hood, is worked in this pattern.

beautiful

pure round wool

of steadfast quality

BACK

Cast on 54 (60, 66, 72, 78, 84) sts.

Work even / straight in patt till Back meas 15³/₄ (16¹/₂, 17¹/₄, 18, 19, 19³/₄)" / 40 (42, 44, 46, 48, 50) cm or length required to armhole.

Shape armholes

Bind / cast off 3 (4, 5, 6, 6, 6) sts at beg of next 2 rows.

Bind / cast off 1 (2, 2, 3, 3, 4) sts at beg of next 2 rows.

Bind / cast off 1 (1, 1, 2, 2, 3) sts at beg of next 2 rows.

Bind / cast off 1 (1, 1, 1, 2, 2) sts at beg of next 2 rows.

Dec 0 (0, 1, 1, 1, 1) st at beg of next 2 rows.

Dec 0 (0, 0, 0, 1, 1) st at beg of next 2 rows [42 (44, 46, 46, 48, 50) sts].

Work even / straight till Back meas 21¹/₄ (22, 23¹/₄, 24, 25¹/₄, 25¹/₂)" / 54 (56, 59, 61, 64, 65) cm.

Shape shoulders

Bind / cast off 3 (4, 4, 4, 4, 4) sts at beg of next 2 rows.

Bind / cast off 3 (3, 3, 3, 3, 4) sts at beg of next 2 rows.

Bind / cast off 3 sts at beg of next 2 rows.

Bind / cast off the rem 24 (24, 26, 26, 28, 28) sts.

LEFT FRONT

Cast on 31 (34, 37, 40, 43, 46) sts.

Work even / straight in patt till Front meas 15³/₄ (16¹/₂, 17¹/₄, 18, 19, 19³/₄)" / 40 (42, 44, 46, 48, 50) cm or length required to armhole.

Shape armholes

Row 1 (RS)   Bind / cast off 3 (4, 5, 6, 6, 6) sts at beg of row.

Row 2 and every even row   Work even / straight.

Row 3   Bind / cast off 1 (2, 2, 3, 3, 4) sts at beg of row.

Row 5   Bind / cast off 1 (1, 1, 2, 2, 3) sts at beg of row.

Row 7   Bind / cast off 1 (1, 1, 1, 2, 2) sts at beg of row.

Row 9   Dec 0 (0, 1, 1, 1, 1) st at beg of row.

Row 11   Dec 0 (0, 0, 0, 1, 1) st at beg of row [25 (26, 27, 27, 28, 29) sts].

Cont even / straight till Front meas 19³/₄ (20¹/₂, 21¹/₂, 22¹/₂, 23¹/₂, 24)" / 50 (52, 55, 57, 60, 61) cm.

Shape neck

Row 1 (WS)   Bind / cast off 7 (7, 8, 8, 9, 9) sts at beg of row.
Row 2, 4 and 6   Work in patt till 2 sts rem, K2tog.
Row 3, 5 and 7   Bind / cast off 2 sts at beg of row [9 (10, 10, 10, 10, 11) sts].

Shape shoulders

Row 1 (RS)   Bind / cast off 3 (4, 4, 4, 4, 4) sts at beg of row.
Row 2 and 4   Work even / straight.
Row 3   Bind / cast off 3 (3, 3, 3, 3, 4) sts at beg of row.

Bind / cast off the rem sts.

RIGHT FRONT

Work as for Left Front, but rev the shapings. **At the same time** make the buttonholes as follows:

Row 9 (RS)   K2, bind / cast off 3, work in patt to end.
Row 10   Work in patt till 2 sts rem, cast on 3, P2.

Make another 5 buttonholes the same way **approximately** every 7¼ (7½, 8, 8¼, 9, 9)" / 18 (19, 20, 21, 23, 23) cm.

To make the buttonhole distance completely accurate, count the rows on your Left Front till bind / cast off at neck. Then deduct 9 rows (to first buttonhole). Deduct 4 rows (above last buttonhole). Divide the rem rows by 5. This equals the number of rows to be worked in between each first buttonhole row.

SLEEVES (both alike)

Cast on 29 (30, 32, 33, 35, 36) sts.

Work even / straight in patt for 10 rows.

Inc 1 st at beg and end of next and every 6th row 12 times till there are 53 (54, 56, 57, 59, 60) sts on needle.

Work even / straight till Sleeve meas 17¾ (17¾, 18, 18, 18, 18½)" / 45 (45, 46, 46, 46, 47) cm.

Shape top

Bind / cast off 3 sts at beg of next 2 rows.

Bind / cast off 2 sts at beg of next 2 (2, 4, 4, 4, 4) rows.

Dec 1 st at beg and end of next and every alt row 9 (9, 9, 9, 10, 10) times.

Bind / cast off 2 sts at beg of next 4 rows.

Next row   (K2tog) 8 (9, 8, 8, 8, 9) times, K1 (0, 0, 1, 1, 0).

Bind / cast off the rem 9 (9, 8, 9, 9, 9) sts.

POCKETS

Cast on 23 sts.

Work in patt for 4½" / 11 cm.

Bind / cast off.

HOOD

Cast on 42 (44, 46, 48, 50, 52) sts.

Work in K1, P1 rib for 2 rows.

Row 3   K1, P1, bind / cast off 2 sts, rib to end.
Row 4   Rib till 2 sts rem, cast on 2 sts, rib 2.

Rib 2 more rows, dec 1 st at end of last row [41 (43, 45, 47, 49, 51) sts].

Work even / straight in patt for 24" / 61 cm, inc 1 st at end of last row.

Work in rib for 6 rows.

Bind / cast off in rib.

BUTTON COVERS

Cast on 6 sts.

Knit 6 rows st st.

Bind / cast off.

FINISHING

Press lightly on wrong side under a damp cloth.

Sew a pocket on each front in desired position.

Join shoulder, side and sleeve seams.

Sew in sleeves.

Turn up and stitch down a ½" / 1 cm hem round lower edge.

Fold Hood in half, RS tog, and join the edge without the buttonhole.

Turn Hood RS out and sew to neck edge, buttonhole on right side.

Cover button moulds with knitted squares, slip st around edge and tighten (discard mould backing).

Sew on buttons to correspond with buttonholes.

EDGES

With the circular needle pick up and knit about 80 (85, 90, 95, 100, 105) sts up right front edge, 104 sts along the hood edge and about 80 (85, 90, 95, 100, 105) sts down left front edge.

Work 1 row of K1, P1 rib.

Bind / cast off in rib.

Tube Hat and Scarf in One

> *A clever all-in-one design for stand-out winter warmth!*

FINISHED MEASUREMENTS

Length 75" / 190 cm

To fit head circumference 20 (21¼, 23)" / 51 (54, 58) cm

MATERIALS

7 (8, 8) 50g balls of Debbie Bliss, Baby Cashmerino in 009 Grey

2 50g balls of Debbie Bliss, Baby Cashmerino in 606 Purple

2 50g balls of Debbie Bliss, Baby Cashmerino in 601 Pink

1 circular needle size 3 US, 24" long / 3.25mm, 60 cm long

1 circular needle size 5 US, 16" long / 3.75mm, 40 cm long

1 circular needle size 5 US, 24" long / 3.75mm, 60 cm long

GAUGE / TENSION

22 sts and 32 rows = 4" / 10 cm in pattern using size 5 US / 3.75mm needle

PATTERN

Rounds 1 and 2 * K9, P1, rep from * to end of round.
Rounds 3 and 4 P1, * K7, P3, rep from * to last 9 sts, K7, P2.
Rounds 5 and 6 P2, * K5, P5, rep from * to last 8 sts, K5, P3.
Rounds 7 and 8 P3, * K3, P7, rep from * to last 7 sts, K3, P4.
Rounds 9 and 10 P4, * K1, P9, rep from * to last 6 sts, K1, P5.
Rounds 11 and 12 As rounds 7 and 8.
Rounds 13 and 14 As rounds 5 and 6.
Rounds 15 and 16 As rounds 3 and 4.
Rounds 17 and 18 As rounds 1 and 2

Rounds 3 to 18 form the patt.

TUBE HAT AND SCARF

With size 3 US / 3.25mm needle and Grey yarn cast on 110 (120, 130) sts.

Work in rounds of K1, P1 rib for 4" / 10 cm.

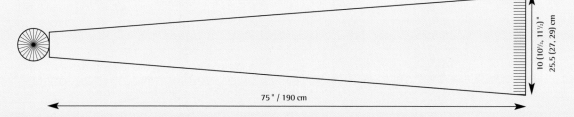

10 (10½, 11½)" / 25.5 (27, 29) cm

75 " / 190 cm

Change to the long size 5 US / 3.75mm needle and Purple yarn and work 6 rounds in st st.

Change to Grey and work 2 rounds in st st.

Change to Purple and work 6 rounds in st st.

Change to Grey and work 40 rounds in patt starting with round 1.

Cont in patt change to Pink and work 6 rounds.

Change to Grey and work 2 rounds in st st.

Change to Pink and work 6 rounds in patt starting with round 1.

Cont in patt change to Grey and work 40 rounds.

Cont in patt change to Purple and work 6 rounds.

Next round Change to Grey and * K9 (10, 11), K2tog, rep from * to end [100 (110, 120) sts].

Next round Work in Grey in st st.

** Change to Purple and work 6 rounds in patt starting with round 1.

Cont in patt change to Grey and work 40 rounds.

Cont in patt change to Pink and work 6 rounds.

Change to Grey and work 2 rounds in st st.

Change to Pink and work 6 rounds in patt starting with round 1.

Cont in patt change to Grey and work 40 rounds.

Cont in patt change to Purple and work 6 rounds. **

Next round Change to Grey and * K8 (9, 10), K2tog, rep from * to end [90 (100, 110) sts].

Next round Work in Grey in st st.

Rep from ** to **

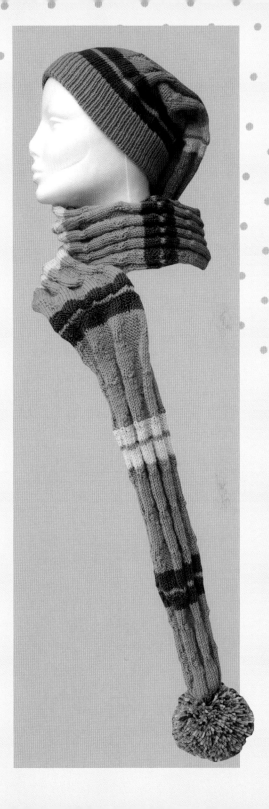

Next round Change to Grey and * K7 (8, 9), K2tog, rep from * to end [80 (90, 100) sts].

Next round Work in Grey in st st.

Rep from ** to **

Next round Change to Grey and * K6 (7, 8), K2tog, rep from * to end [70 (80, 90) sts].

Next round Work in Grey in st st.

Rep from ** to **

Next round Change to the short size 5 US / 3.75mm needle and Grey and * K5 (6, 7), K2tog, rep from * to end [60 (70, 80) sts].

Next round Work in Grey in st st.

Rep from ** to **

Next round Change to Grey and * K4 (5, 6), K2tog, rep from * to end [50 (60, 70) sts].

Next round Work in Grey in st st.

Change to Purple and work 6 rounds in patt starting with round 1.

Cont in patt change to Grey and work 40 rounds.

Next round K2tog all round.

Thread yarn through all sts, tighten and fasten off.

FINISHING

Press work lightly on wrong side.

Fold the rib in half and slip st to inside.

Using 4 strands of Grey and one strand each of Purple and Pink make a 3¹/₂" / 9 cm diameter pompon and sew on.

1950

Waved Cable-Pattern Sweater

Dream of sea breezes in this cosy sweater with its waved design.

FINISHED MEASUREMENTS

To fit bust 32 (34, 36, 38, 40, 42)" / 81 (86, 91, 97, 102, 107) cm

Length 20½ (21, 21¼, 21½, 22, 22½)" / 52 (53, 54, 55, 56, 57) cm

Sleeve seam length 17¾ (17¾, 18, 18, 18, 18½)" / 45 (45, 46, 46, 46, 47) cm

MATERIALS

2 250g cones of Yeoman Yarns, Cannele Corded Mercerised Cotton 4 Ply in 5 Skye.

1 pair size 2 US / 2.75mm needles

1 pair size 3 US / 3.25mm needles

1 cable stitch needle size 2 US / 2.75mm

1 circular needle size 2 US, 16" long / 2.75mm, 40 cm long

1 stitch holder

GAUGE / TENSION

32 sts and 32 rows = 4" / 10 cm in pattern using size 3 US / 3.25mm needles

ABBREVIATIONS

Cable 8 = sl next 4 sts onto cable needle and keep at front of work, K next 4 sts, K4 sts from cable needle.

PATTERN (divisible by 30 +2 sts)

X = number of times pattern is to be repeated in the different sizes (see garment instructions).

Row 1 (RS) (P2, K6, P2, K20) X times, P2.

Row 2 (K2, P20, K2, P6) X times, K2.

Row 3 (P2, M1, K6, M1, P2, K2tog, K16, sl 1, K1, psso) X times, P2.

Row 4 (K2, P18, K2, P8) X times, K2.

Row 5 (P2, M1, K8, M1, P2, K2tog, K14, sl 1, K1, psso) X times, P2.

Row 6 (K2, P16, K2, P10) X times, K2.

Row 7 (P2, M1, K10, M1, P2, K2tog, K12, sl 1, K1, psso) X times, P2.

Row 8 (K2, P14, K2, P12) X times, K2.

Row 9 (P2, M1, K12, M1, P2, K2tog, K10, sl 1, K1, psso) X times, P2.

Row 10 (K2, P12, K2, P14) X times, K2.

Row 11 (P2, M1, K14, M1, P2, K2tog, K8, sl 1, K1, psso) X times, P2.

Row 12 (K2, P10, K2, P16) X times, K2.

Row 13 (P2, M1, K16, M1, P2, K2tog, K6, sl 1, K1, psso) X times, P2.

1937

Row 14 (K2, P8, K2, P18) X times, K2.

Row 15 (P2, M1, K18, M1, P2, K2tog, K4, sl 1, K1, psso) X times, P2.

Row 16 (K2, P6, K2, P20) X times, K2.

Row 17 (P2, K2, Cable 8, Cable 8, K2, P2, K6) X times, P2.

Row 18 As row 16.

Row 19 (P2, K20, P2, K6) X times, P2.

Rep last two rows twice (will be rows 20, 21, 22, 23).

Rep rows 16, 17, 16 (will be rows 24, 25, 26).

Row 27 (P2, K2tog, K16, sl 1, K1, psso, P2, M1, K6, M1) X times, P2.

Row 28 As row 14.

Row 29 (P2, K2tog, K14, sl 1, K1, psso, P2, M1, K8, M1) X times, P2.

Row 30 As row 12.

Row 31 (P2, K2tog, K12, sl 1, K1, psso, P2, M1, K10, M1) X times, P2.

Row 32 As row 10.

Row 33 (P2, K2tog, K10, sl 1, K1, psso, P2, M1, K12, M1) X times, P2.

Row 34 As row 8.

Row 35 (P2, K2tog, K8, sl 1, K1, psso, P2, M1, K14, M1) X times, P2.

Row 36 As row 6.

Row 37 (P2, K2tog, K6, sl 1, K1, psso, P2, M1, K16, M1) X times, P2.

Row 38 As row 4.

Row 39 (P2, K2tog, K4, sl 1, K1, psso, P2, M1, K18, M1) X times, P2.

Row 40 As row 2.

Row 41 (P2, K6, P2, K2, Cable 8, Cable 8, K2) X times, P2.

Row 42 As row 2.

Rep rows 1 and 2 three times (will be rows 43, 44, 45, 46, 47, 48).

Row 49 As row 41.

FRONT AND BACK (both alike)

With size 2 US / 2.75mm needles cast on 110 (118, 126, 134, 142, 150) sts.

Work in K1, P1 rib for 3" / 8 cm.

Inc in last row by knitting twice into every 5th (5th, 6th, 6th, 7th, 7th) st till 0 (18, 6, 2, 2, 10) sts rem, rib 0 (18, 6, 2, 2, 10) sts [132 (138, 146, 156, 162, 170) sts].

Change to size 3 US / 3.25mm needles and work in patt. To make up for the odd sts in the different sizes, work as follows on the Front and Back:

Uneven rows (RS) P2, K3 (6, 10, 0, 3, 7), (Pattern) 4 (4, 4, 5, 5, 5) times, P2, K3 (6, 10, 0, 3, 7), P2.

Even rows K2, P3 (6, 10, 0, 3, 7), (Pattern) 4 (4, 4, 5, 5, 5) times, K2, P3 (6, 10, 0, 3, 7), K2.

Cont in patt from row 3 till work meas $13\frac{1}{2}$ ($13\frac{3}{4}$, $13\frac{3}{4}$, $14\frac{1}{4}$, $14\frac{1}{4}$, $14\frac{1}{2}$)" / 34 (35, 35, 36, 36, 37) cm.

Shape armholes

(RS) Cont in patt and bind / cast off 4 (5, 5, 6, 6, 7) sts at beg of first 2 rows.

Bind / cast off 3 (3, 3, 4, 4, 4) sts at beg of next 2 rows.

Bind / cast off 2 sts at beg of next 2 rows.

K2tog at beg and end of next and every alt rows till there are 106 (108, 112, 114, 118, 122) sts on needle.

Cont even / straight in patt till work meas $14\frac{1}{4}$ ($15\frac{1}{2}$, $15\frac{3}{4}$, $16\frac{1}{4}$, $16\frac{1}{2}$, 17)" / 36 (39, 40, 41, 42, 43) cm.

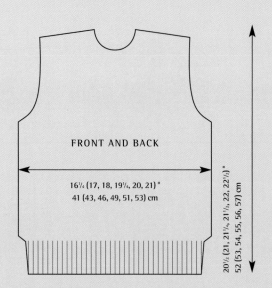

FRONT AND BACK

16¼ (17, 18, 19¼, 20, 21) "
41 (43, 46, 49, 51, 53) cm

20½ (21, 21¼, 21½, 22, 22½) "
52 (53, 54, 55, 56, 57) cm

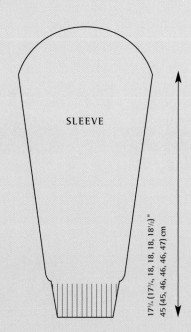

SLEEVE

17¼ (17¼, 18, 18, 18½) "
45 (45, 46, 46, 47) cm

Shape neck and shoulders

Row 1 (RS) Knit 46 sts in patt and slip rem sts onto st holder. Turn.

Cont in patt and bind / cast off 2 sts at neck side 7 times and then bind / cast off 8 sts at armhole side 4 times.

Join yarn to other side.

Bind / cast off 14 (16, 20, 22, 26, 30) sts and work in patt to end.

Cont working as for first side of neck and shoulders, but rev the shapings.

SLEEVES (both alike)

With size 2 US / 2.75mm needles cast on 62 (62, 68, 70, 70, 74) sts and work in K1, P1 rib for 3" / 8 cm.

Change to size 3 US / 3.25mm needles and work in patt. To make up for the odd sts in the different sizes, work as follows on the Sleeves:

Row 1 (RS) P0 (0, 2, 2, 2, 2), K0 (0, 1, 2, 2, 4), (Pattern) 2 times, P2, K0 (0, 1, 2, 2, 4), P0 (0, 2, 2, 2, 2).
Row 2 K0 (0, 2, 2, 2, 2), P0 (0, 1, 2, 2, 4), (Pattern) 2 times, K2, P0 (0, 1, 2, 2, 4), K0 (0, 2, 2, 2, 2).

Cont in patt and inc at beg and end of every 8th row till there are 90 (90, 94, 96, 98, 100) sts on needle. Work the extra sts into the patt, but maintain a border of P0 (0, 2, 2, 2, 2), K0 (0, 1, 2, 2, 4) on either side.

Cont even / straight till Sleeve meas 17³/₄ (17³/₄, 18, 18, 18, 18¹/₂)" / 45 (45, 46, 46, 46, 47) cm.

Shape top

Cont in patt (without the border) and bind /cast off 4 (4, 5, 5, 6, 6) sts at beg of first 2 rows.

Bind / cast off 3 (3, 3, 4, 4, 4) sts at beg of next 2 rows.

Bind / cast off 2 sts at beg of next 2 rows.

K2tog at beg and end of next and every alt rows till there are 30 sts on needle.

Bind / cast off.

Join shoulder seams.

COLLAR

Using circular needle pick up and knit 130 (134, 142, 146, 154, 162) sts round neck edge.

Work in K1, P1 rib for 30 rows.

Bind / cast off.

Turn in ribbing and stitch edge to first row of rib.

FINISHING

Join side and sleeve seams.

Sew in sleeves.

Angora Bolero

Soft flattery for frosty nights and dress-up afternoons.

FINISHED MEASUREMENTS

To fit bust 32 (34, 36, 38, 40, 42)" / 81 (86, 91, 97, 102, 107) cm

Back length from top of shoulder 12½ (12½, 13, 13, 13½, 13½)" / 32 (32, 33, 33, 34, 34) cm

MATERIALS

2 (2, 3, 3, 4, 4) 50g balls of Orkney Angora, 100% Angora 4 ply in 21 Cerise

1 pair size 2 US / 2.75mm needles

1 pair size 3 US / 3.25mm needles

1 circular needle size 2 US, 32" long / 2.75mm, 80 cm long

GAUGE / TENSION

30 sts and 40 rows = 4" / 10 cm in st st using size 3 US / 3.25mm needles

BOLERO (worked in st st)

With size 3 US / 3.25mm needles cast on 106 (114, 122, 130, 138, 146) sts to form lower back edge.

Working in st st, inc 1 st at beg and end of next and every alt row 8 times.

Inc 1 st at beg and end of every row 27 times [176 (184, 192, 200, 208, 216) sts.]

Cast on 4 sts at beg of next 26 rows [280 (288, 296, 304, 312, 320) sts].

Work 46 (46, 50, 50, 54, 54) rows even / straight.

Next row (RS) K125 (128, 131, 134, 137, 140), bind / cast off 30 (32, 34, 36, 38, 40), K to end.

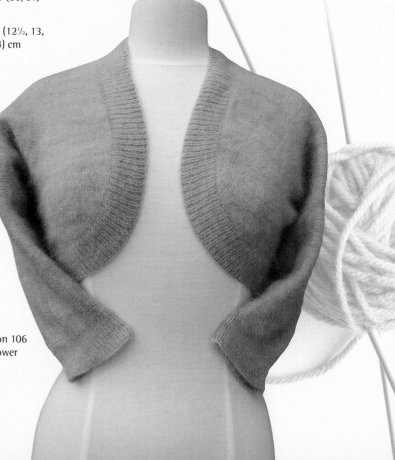

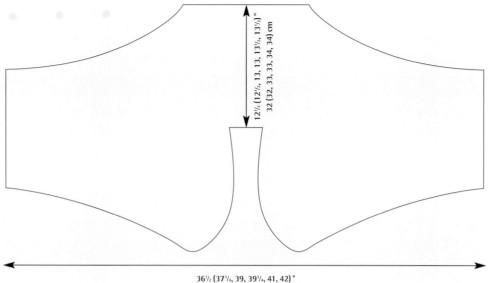

12½ (12½, 13, 13, 13½, 13½) "
32 (32, 33, 33, 34, 34) cm

36½ (37¾, 39, 39¾, 41, 42) "
93 (96, 99, 101, 104, 107) cm

Work on the last group of 125 (128, 131, 134, 137, 140) sts.

At **front edge** inc 1 st on every 12th row 3 (3, 4, 4, 5, 5) times. There will be 128 (131, 135, 138, 142, 145) sts on needle and 48 (48, 52, 52, 56, 56) rows worked from bind / cast off for neck.

At **sleeve edge** bind / cast off 4 sts at beg of next and every alt row 12 times more; dec 1 st at sleeve edge on every row 27 times; dec 1 st at sleeve edge on next and every alt row 8 times.

At **the same time** cont inc at front edge on every 12th row 2 (2, 1, 1, 0, 0) more times till there are 5 inc; dec 1 st every 5th row 4 times; dec 1 st every 5th and 6th row 4 times; bind / cast off 3 sts; bind / cast off 3 (3, 3, 3, 3, 4) sts; bind / cast off 4 (4, 4, 4, 5, 5) sts; bind / cast off 5 (5, 5, 6, 7, 8) sts; bind / cast off 5 (6, 7, 8, 8, 8) sts; bind / cast off 5 (6, 7, 8, 8, 9) sts; bind / cast off 6 (7, 8, 8, 9, 9) sts.

Rejoin yarn to sts on needle (at neck edge) and work to match first side.

RIBBING

With size 2 US / 2.75mm needles and RS of work facing pick up and knit 106 (114, 122, 130, 138, 146) sts across lower edge of back.

Row 1 K2, * P1, K1, rep from * to end.

Rep this row 17 times.

Bind / cast off in rib.

With the circular needle and starting at lower edge of Right Front with RS facing pick up and knit 125 (128, 135, 138, 145, 148) sts along Right Front, 30 (32, 34, 36, 38, 40) sts across back of neck, and 125 (128, 135, 138, 145, 148) sts along Left Front [280 (288, 304, 312, 328, 336) sts].

Work back and forth on the needle.

Row 1 K2, * P1, K1, rep from * to end.

Rep this row 17 times.

Bind / cast off in rib.

Angora Bolero

CUFFS (both alike)

With size 2 US / 2.75mm needles and RS of work facing pick up and knit 80 (80, 84, 84, 88, 88) sts along wrist edge.

Row 1 K2, * P1, K1, rep from * to end.

Rep this row 17 times.

Bind / cast off in rib.

FINISHING

With RS of work facing, block fabric by pinning out around edges and steam with iron 1" / 2.5 cm above surface.

Join side / sleeve seams.

Press seams lightly.

1950

Techniques and Abbreviations

Difficulty

Easy Knitting

For knitters with some experience.

For experienced knitters.

Gauge / Tension

Before starting any garment, you should always work a tension sample. It is important you obtain the right tension otherwise your finished garment can be misshapen.

When measuring, lay the knitted piece on a flat smooth surface such as a table and let it 'relax'.

If your square is bigger than stated in the pattern, try a smaller needle size.

If your square is smaller than required, try a larger needle size.

Tassels (right below)

1. Wrap yarn loosely around a piece of cardboard till tassel is desired thickness.

2. Thread one strand (or more) of yarn through the top and tie firmly, leaving a long end for winding and sewing.

3. Cut the yarn at the bottom of the cardboard.

4. Hide the knot, and the short end left from tying it, under the folded strands.

5. Wind the long strand around the top of the tassel a few times to secure the folded end, then thread it through so that it comes out at the top.

6. Trim ends.

Abbreviations

The following abbreviations are those in general use throughout this book. If, in any pattern, an abbreviation occurs which is applicable to that pattern only, details are given at the beginning of the instructions.

If there is a difference between US and UK terminology, the US terminology is followed by the UK equivalent.

* (asterisk) = repetition. The instructions written after * or between two *s have to be repeated to the end of the row, or the number of times stated. For example: * K1, P1, rep from * 3 times, means that you have to repeat the K1, P1 3 times after having done it once; that is, 4 times in all.

(....) Repeat instructions inside brackets as many times as indicated after brackets.

alt = alternate

beg = begin(ning)

bind off (US) = cast off (UK)

cm = centimetres

cont = continue(ing)

dec = decrease(ing)

even (US) = straight (UK)

foll = follow(ing)

g = gram(s)

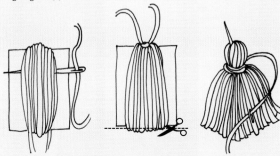

Techniques and Abbreviations

gauge (US) = tension (UK)

g-st = garter stitch (K every row)

inc = increase(ing)

" = inches

K = knit

K2tog = knit two stitches together

K-b = knit-back (insert needle through back of loop)

K-b2 tog = knit-back two stitches together

kw = knitwise, i.e. inserting the point of the right-hand needle into the front of the stitch and out at the back, as if to knit.

M1 = make one: Pick up horizontal bar lying before next stitch and knit into back of it.

M1 pw = make one purlwise: Pick up horizontal bar lying before next stitch and purl into back of it.

meas = measures

mm = millimetres

P = purl

patt = pattern(s)

P2tog = purl two stitches together

psso = pass slipped stitch over: Lift the slipped stitch over the next knitted stitch and off needle.

pw = purlwise, i.e. inserting the point of the right-hand needle into the front part of the stitch from the back and out at the front, as if to purl.

rem = remain(ing)

rep = repeat

rev = reverse(ing)

rev st st = reverse stockinette stitch / reverse stocking stitch. Row 1 (RS) P. Row 2 K.

RS = Right Side

sl = slip. Instead of knitting or purling the next stitch, simply transfer it to the right-hand needle.

st(s) = stitch(es)

st st = stockinette stitch (US) / stocking stitch (UK). Row 1 (RS) K. Row 2 P.

tbl = through back of loop(s)

tog = together

WS = Wrong Side

yb = yarn back: Bring the yarn to the back of work.

yfd = yarn forward: Bring the yarn to the front of work.

yo / yon = yarn over (US) / yarn over needle (UK). This is used between a P and a K st.

yo / yrn = yarn over (US) / yarn round needle (UK). This is used between a K and a P st.

Crochet abbreviations

ch = chain

sl st = slip stitch

sc / dc = single crochet (US) / double crochet (UK)

dc / tr = double crochet (US) / treble crochet (UK)

Suppliers

USA
To find your nearest supplier, contact:

Capricorn Yarns
3 Millside
Brampton
Cumbria CA8 9JU
Tel: 011 44 1228 670 774
E: info@capricorn-yarns.com
www.capricorn-mohair.com

Debbie Bliss
Knitting Fever Inc.
315 Bayview Avenue
Amityville, NY 11701
Tel: 516 546 3600
Fax: 516 546 6871
E: admin@knittingfever.com
www.knittingfever.com

Farrlacey Alpacas
Main Road
Wood Enderby
Lincolnshire PE22 7PQ
Tel: 011 44 1507 568 249
E: sales@farrlacey.co.uk
www.farrlacey.co.uk

Jamieson and Smith Yarns
Schoolhouse Press
Tel: 800 968-5648
Fax: 715 884-2829
E: info@schoolhousepress.com
www.schoolhousepress.com
OR
Yarns International
PO Box 467
Cabin John
MD 20818-0467
Tel: 800 927-6728
Fax: 301 229-4204
E: info@yarnsinternational.com
www.yarnsinternational.com

Suppliers

Orkney Angora
Upper Breckan
Isle of Sanday
Orkney KW17 2AZ
Tel: 011 44 1857 600 421
E: info@orkneyangora.co.uk
www.orkneyangora.co.uk

Rowan/Jaeger/RYC
www.knitrowan.com

Twilleys
www.twilleysofstamford.co.uk

Yeoman Yarns
Cardiknits
92 Cardinal Drive
Hamilton
Ontario
Canada LA9 4H7
E: cardiknits@sympatico.ca
www.cardiknits.com
OR
Love Lisa Handknits
1105 Heiden Court
Flower Mound, TX 75028
Tel: 682 554-0313
E: lisa@lovelisa.us
www.lovelisa.us

UK
To find your nearest supplier, contact:

Capricorn Yarns
3 Millside
Brampton
Cumbria CA8 9JU
Tel: 01228 670 774
E: info@capricorn-yarns.com
www.capricorn-mohair.com

Debbie Bliss
www.designeryarns.uk.com
or
www.debbieblissonline.com

Farrlacey Alpacas
Main Road
Wood Enderby
Lincolnshire PE22 7PQ
Tel: 01507 568 249
E: sales@farrlacey.co.uk
www.farrlacey.co.uk

Jamieson and Smith
90 North Road
Lerwick
Shetland Islands
Tel: 01595 693 579
Fax: 01595 695 009
E: sales@shetlandwoolbrokers.co.uk
www.shetland-wool-brokers.zetnet.co.uk

Orkney Angora
Upper Breckan
Isle of Sanday
Orkney KW17 2AZ
Tel: 01857 600 421
E: info@orkneyangora.co.uk
www.orkneyangora.co.uk

Rowan/Jaeger/RYC
www.knitrowan.com

Twilleys
www.twilleysofstamford.co.uk

Yeoman Yarns
36 Churchill Way
Fleckney
Leicester LE8 8UD
Tel: 01162 402 522
E: sales@yeomanyarns.co.uk
www.yeoman-yarns.co.uk

HABERDASHERY

MacCulloch & Wallis
25–26 Dering Street
London W1S 1AT
Tel: 02076 290 311
www.macculloch-wallis.co.uk

POMPON KIT

Texere Yarns
College Mill
Barkerend Road
Bradford BD1 4AU
Tel: 01274 722 191
www.texereyarns.co.uk

Acknowledgments

This book could not have been created without help from a lot of people. I am indebted to all my friends and family who have stood by me and encouraged me on the way. A special thank you to the ladies who contributed their treasured vintage patterns, especially Alix Hoff and Joan Muirhead; to Quintin Tudor Evans and Anna Levene for professional advice; to my wonderful knitters, Brenda Jennings, Alice Walker and Frances Coote, who have helped me decipher the old patterns and make them into modern garments; to Maggie Partington-Smith and Bridget Tudor Evans for period design knowledge; to John Peacock for his enthusiasm and for introducing me to Thames & Hudson; and to my boyfriend, Jim Hoff, for all his loving help, patience and tolerance all the way through.

Credits

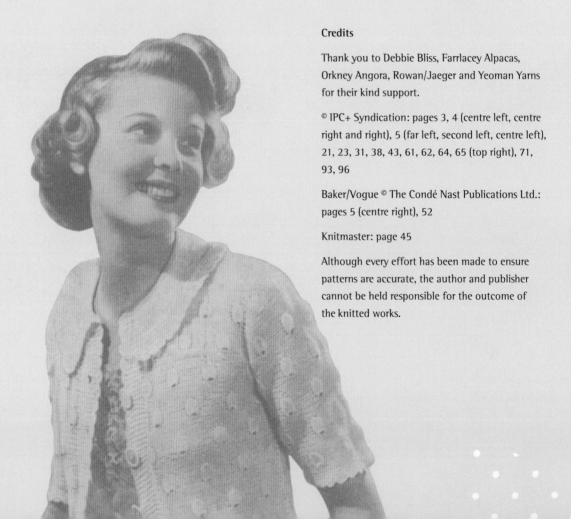